Diversifying the Faculty

A Guidebook for Search Committees

Caroline Sotello Viernes Turner

 ASSOCIATION OF AMERICAN COLLEGES & UNIVERSITIES

Published by the
Association of American Colleges and Universities
1818 R Street, NW
Washington, DC 20009
202.387.3760
www.aacu.org

ISBN 0-911696-90-3

To order additional copies of this publication or to find out about other AAC&U
publications, e-mail pub_desk@aacu.org or call 202.387.3760.

Table of Contents

PREFACE v

ACKNOWLEDGMENTS vii

INTRODUCTION 1

PART 1: BEFORE THE SEARCH BEGINS 5
   Communicating the educational rationale
   Aligning departmental and institutional commitments
   Creating a welcoming environment
   Securing resources
   Countering segregated networks

PART 2: THE SEARCH PROCESS 13
   Forming the search committee
   Educating the search committee on personnel issues
   Debunking the myths
   Creating the position description
   Attracting a diverse candidate pool
   Examining hiring biases
   Hosting the campus visit
   Making the offer

PART 3: AFTER THE SEARCH 23
   Supporting the new hire
   Assessing the search process and outcome
   A final note

APPENDICES 29
   A: Checklist of best practices
   B: Leading Ph.D. institutions of minority Ph.D.s, 1993-1997
   C: Baccalaureate institutions identified as women doctorate productivity leaders
   D: Web resources of programs for building diverse faculties

NOTES 37

REFERENCES 39

ANNOTATED BIBLIOGRAPHY 43

Preface

This monograph, *Diversifying the Faculty: A Guidebook for Search Committees*, addresses only one aspect of a much larger issue that the Association of American Colleges and Universities has made a centerpiece of its programming for more than a decade. Overcoming its own legacies of exclusion, how can higher education now tap the rich diversity within the United States as an educational and civic resource? AAC&U's signature initiative, *American Commitments: Diversity, Democracy, and Liberal Learning*, which involved more than 300 colleges and universities, both illuminated and fostered a virtual transformation in institutional practices, curricular and co-curricular structures, and campus life at colleges across the nation. Diversity increasingly became not a problem to be dealt with but an essential component of intellectual inquiry, a means of enhancing student learning, and a measure of our nation's commitment to its democratic principles.

Influenced by growing evidence that diversity enriches students' intellectual, moral, and civic development, academic institutions have been asserting their determination to bring racial and ethnic diversity not simply to the admissions office or the curriculum, but to the lectern and the laboratory. Yet, despite stunning progress in diversifying the collegiate student body over the past four decades, the progress in diversifying the faculty has been discouraging. This guide aims to remedy that. AAC&U is convinced that the majority of colleges and universities want to diversify their faculties racially and ethnically, but don't always know how. This deliberately concise monograph seeks to articulate various elements of a successful search. The recommendations in this monograph are informed by the research of scholars who have sought to shed light on the seemingly intractable obstacles to successful searches. The good news in *Diversifying the Faculty* is that many of these barriers can be overcome—and overcome quickly. There are concrete, immediate steps that institutions can take to increase the racial and ethnic diversity within their faculty. And search committees are key instruments in accomplishing that feat.

Recognizing that the search committee functions in a larger context, the volume suggests ways the institution can facilitate the work of the committee long before a candidate ever steps foot on campus for an interview. It then not only takes the committee on a step by step process to improve the likelihood of a successful search, but also recommends items to consider after a hire is confirmed to ensure the new faculty member will be more likely to stay. Designed as a compendium of additional resources for a search committee, the appendix includes an expansive annotated bibliography for more in-depth study of various aspects of a search, Web site resources to help expand the pool of potential candidates, and tables indicating undergraduate and graduate schools with exemplary histories of producing U.S. graduates of color with doctorates.

AAC&U is fortunate to have persuaded Dr. Caroline Sotello Viernes Turner, one of the most distinguished scholars in this field, to author this monograph. We hope *Diversifying the Faculty* helps colleges and universities come to a better understanding of how they might organize a successful search, and in that process enable the academy to meet its obligation to produce graduates equipped to be informed, responsible citizens in a world where diversity is a given but full equality still an aspiration.

Caryn McTighe Musil
Vice President, Diversity,
Equity, and Global Initiatives
Association of American
Colleges and Universities

Acknowledgments

I want to acknowledge the invaluable help of AAC&U's National Advisory Panel which met in the early stages of this project to define some of the key questions, suggest overarching frameworks, and advise me periodically during the course of the project. The members of that panel include: Jonathan Alger, then Counsel to the American Association of University Professors and now Associate General Counsel, University of Michigan; Jerry Gaff, AAC&U's Senior Scholar and Co-Director of AAC&U's Preparing Future Faculty program; Hector Garza, then Executive Director of Minorities in Higher Education Program at the American Council on Education and now President of the National Council for Community and Education Partnerships; Debra Humphreys, AAC&U's Vice President for Communications and Public Affairs; Caryn McTighe Musil, AAC&U's Vice President for Diversity, Equity, and Global Initiatives; Daryl Smith, Professor, Claremont Graduate University; Orlando Taylor, Professor and Dean, Graduate College, Howard University; and Ric Weibl, then AAC&U Director of Programs, Office of Education and Institutional Renewal and now Editor at the American Association for the Advancement of Science.

I also want to recognize two graduate assistants, Leslie Lydell from the University of Minnesota and Laura Love from Arizona State University, for their support on the monograph in its various stages. Diana Alvarado, AAC&U's Project Assistant, also provided critical help with some initial research.

As the manuscript evolved, I also turned to colleagues, such as Dr. Patricia Hyer, Associate Provost for Academic Administration at Virginia Tech University, and many others across the country whose thoughts are sprinkled throughout this manuscript. Some of these contributions were made in confidence, so I cannot acknowledge by name all of those who assisted with this project. Even though your names have been omitted, my deepest appreciation goes to each of you.

Finally, I want to acknowledge people at AAC&U who shepherded the manuscript through the final stages of publication. I want to thank Alma Clayton-Pedersen, Vice President of the Office of Education and Institutional Renewal; Michelle Asha Cooper, Program Associate in the Office of Diversity, Equity, and Global Initiatives, who devoted countless hours and much of her energy reserves to conducting research, editing, and proofing this manuscript; Maria Figueroa and Amanda Lepof, also of the same office, who provided invaluable administrative and technical support to this project; Jerry Gaff, who always saw the connection between this monograph and the goals of Preparing Future Faculty; and Caryn McTighe Musil, who first conceived of this monograph and stayed involved with the manuscript from beginning to end. In AAC&U's editorial office, I want to thank David Tritelli, whose exquisite editing skill transformed the manuscript, and Julie Warren, who oversaw the design and production of *Diversifying the Faculty: A Guidebook for Search Committees*.

I gratefully acknowledge support for this project from the Pew Charitable Trusts and the Ford Foundation.

As in all things I have accomplished, I want to recognize the importance of the inspirational and supportive contributions of my family, my friends, and my faith. You have stood by me through the years.

Caroline Sotello Viernes Turner

Introduction

America's colleges and universities are educating a larger and more diverse group of students than ever before. According to a recent study conducted by the Educational Testing Service, an even greater transformation in the student body will occur over the next decade. By 2015, for example, 80 percent of the anticipated 2.6 million new college students will be African American, Hispanic, Asian/Pacific Islander, or American Indian. Nationwide, the number of undergraduate minority students enrolled in colleges and universities will increase from 29.4 percent to 37.2 percent. The number of minority students in the District of Columbia, California, Hawaii, and New Mexico will exceed the number of white students. In Texas, the campus population of minorities will be nearly 50 percent, and in New York, Maryland, Florida, New Jersey, Louisiana, and Mississippi, minority student enrollment is expected to exceed 40 percent of the total undergraduate population (Carnavale and Fry 2000).

While we have witnessed steady growth in the racial and ethnic diversity of the student population, we have not seen similar diversification among college faculty. Despite the efforts of many colleges and universities, racial and ethnic minorities remain grossly underrepresented among the faculty; they make up only 13.8 percent of the total faculty nationwide. The latest annual status report,

Minorities in Higher Education, indicates the proportion among full-time faculty: 5 percent African Americans (non-Hispanic), 2.7 percent Hispanics, 5.7 percent Asian Americans, and 0.4 percent American Indians (Harvey 2001).

While we have witnessed steady growth in the racial and ethnic diversity of the student population, we have not seen similar diversification among college faculty.

Moreover, faculty of color[1] are not evenly distributed across institutional types, disciplines, or academic ranks. For instance, larger numbers of Hispanic faculty are employed at two-year institutions. African Americans, American Indians, and Hispanics are most acutely underrepresented in the fields of science and engineering. Across ranks, Asian Americans comprise only 1.8 percent of academic administrators (Turner and Myers 2000; Harvey 2001).

The arguments for faculty diversity are as compelling as the arguments for student diversity, which also extend beyond the obvious reasons of equity. Faculty diversification contributes directly to educational quality. A diverse faculty means better educational outcomes for *all* students. To serve current and future student populations, multiple and diverse perspectives are needed at every level of college teaching and governance. The more diverse college and university faculty are, the more likely it is that all students will be exposed to a wider range of scholarly perspectives and to ideas drawn from a variety of life experiences. The emergence within the last thirty years of new bodies of knowledge can be attributed to the diverse backgrounds and interests of faculty of color. By bringing new research questions and fresh perspectives to the academic enterprise, these scholars create intellectual stimulation for both students and faculty alike (Turner 2000; *Shattering the Silences* 1997).

Although the pool of minority faculty is underdeveloped, studies have shown that it is also underutilized.

To better serve new students and to prepare all students for an increasingly diverse world, it is important that colleges and universities transform not only what they teach but also how they teach. Evidence suggests that exposure in college to a diverse faculty along with diversified curricula and teaching methods produces students who are more complex thinkers, more confident in traversing cultural differences, and more likely to seek to remedy inequities after graduation (Hurtado et al. 1999; Smith and Associates 1997). Since faculty of color are frequently those who take scholarship and teaching in new directions, their presence on campus makes this goal easier to attain. In fact, faculty of color surpass their white

colleagues in the use of teaching techniques associated with student-centered pedagogy (antonio 1999). Furthermore, faculty of color provide students with diverse role models and help provide more effective mentoring to minority students.

The current professoriat, largely white and male, is now preparing to retire. The young professors hired in large numbers during the academic boom years of the 1960s are near the end of their careers. This pending wave of retirements will profoundly affect higher education in the coming years, and faculty and administrators at many institutions are hopeful that these anticipated vacancies will be filled with faculty of color.

Although the pool of minority faculty is underdeveloped, studies have shown that it is also underutilized (Turner and Myers 2000; Smith, Wolf, and Busenberg 1996). Moreover, within the higher education community, myths and misconceptions dominate the conversation about the recruitment of faculty of color. It is often asserted, for example, that potential applicants are unqualified, widely sought after, or unavailable. It is important that campuses move beyond such mistaken notions. These myths, stereotypes, and assumptions help maintain the status quo and create significant barriers to achieving a racially and ethnically diverse faculty.

Informed by the growing research literature on racial and ethnic diversity in the faculty, this guidebook offers specific recommendations to faculty search committees. Many of these recommendations are also based on first-hand observations, testimonials, and conversations with faculty of color[2]. The primary goal of this guidebook is to help structure and execute successful searches for faculty of color.

Although focused on junior-level faculty searches, many of the recommendations also can be applied across ranks and disciplinary lines. Of course, the specific procedures for conducting the search process will vary from institution to institution, but the analyses and suggested actions presented here are widely applicable.

This guidebook is divided into three parts, mirroring the steps in the faculty hiring process. *Part I: Before the Search Begins* describes the necessary and ongoing campus processes that are crucial in creating a context within which search committees can successfully diversify the faculty. *Part II: The Search Process* details what should happen during the search to promote success in hiring faculty of color. Since recruiting faculty of color without retaining them is self-defeating, *Part III: After the Search* includes suggested actions to be taken after the search is concluded. Best and promising hiring practices from a variety of institutions are interspersed throughout the text, and an extensive annotated bibliography and several appendices are included to help search committees and institutional leaders in this important challenge: diversifying the racial and ethnic composition of the faculty.

Before the Search Begins

The faculty searches most likely to contribute to the goal of diversifying the faculty are those conducted in the context of an ongoing, institution-wide commitment to faculty diversity. Discussed below are five institutional steps to be taken in advance of any particular faculty search:

- Communicating the educational rationale
- Aligning departmental and institutional commitments
- Creating a welcoming environment
- Securing resources
- Countering segregated networks

These steps fall outside the mandate of a particular search committee and ought to be undertaken by the full spectrum of campus leaders. They are included here, however, because committee members should be aware of the benefits and challenges of the institutional context within which they work. The importance of these steps is clearly manifest during a search. Therefore, the search committee process can reveal gaps in a campus's commitment to diversity, and committee members can become agents for change on campus.

1. Communicating the Educational Rationale

The educational missions of most colleges and universities recognize the value of diversity—in their student body, faculty, and staff—as vitally important to preparing students to live and work in a world marked by sweeping demographic changes and global interconnectedness. A good way for institutions to strengthen their commitment to diversity is to explicitly incorporate faculty diversity as a goal within an overall strategic plan for preparing graduates to be culturally competent global citizens. The more successful search committees believe that racial and ethnic diversity both meets the programmatic needs of the department and advances the institution's overall mission.

Rendering explicit the connection between faculty diversity and educational quality encourages the campus as a whole—including, more specifically, departments and search committees—to commit to the spirit of the goal. It can also contribute to the creation of a welcoming campus environment for faculty of color and encourage the closer alignment of departmental and institutional commitments to diversity. Institutional leaders can create a wide variety of opportunities for communicating the educational rationale for faculty diversity. Below are some suggestions for generating campus discussions:

- Encourage each department to have a forum or a roundtable discussion that examines the racial composition of doctorates in their discipline and couple that discussion with research findings on the impact of hiring faculty of color.

- Arrange to show *Shattering the Silences: Minority Professors Break into the Ivory Tower* (see annotated bibliography) to the department and organize follow-up discussions.

- Invite leading researchers who have expertise in the area of faculty diversity to present findings to the college as a whole.

- Devote part of the college's annual retreat or faculty symposium to a presentation on national research that compares faculty across race, gender, nationality, and other factors. Build discussion groups around implications of findings.

- Ask each department to do its own racial audit of hiring patterns over the last ten years and track some of the consequences to curriculum, teaching, and scholarship that resulted.

- Through a college teaching and learning center, offer designated forums or workshops on pedagogy that offer cross-racial and cross-cultural comparisons of teaching profiles. Discuss the implications.

- Organize a forum with communities of color near the college in which you explore the ways in which higher education could more effectively examine our nation's racial legacies. Discuss this group's perception of your campus's commitment to diversity.

- Conduct inter-group dialogue sessions with students to discuss their perceptions of the faculty's racial composition and its effect on their learning.

2. Aligning Departmental and Institutional Commitments

Departmental searches can resonate far beyond the more limited borders of a given department. A faculty search can, in fact, become a measure of larger institutional commitments and attitudes. As E. Gordon Gee, former president of Ohio State University, recognizes, an institution's core values surface during a search process. "While the goal of the search is, of course, to attract outstanding individuals to our Ohio State family, there are broader implications of the search process as well," Gee points out. "There are few activities in which we engage that have more powerful public impact than searches. Every search committee leaves in its wake literally hundreds of candidates whose impression of Ohio State will be based largely on the courtesy, timeliness, and professionalism of our communications. Furthermore, the way searches are conducted speaks volumes about our individual and institutional values" (Office of Human Resources and Office of Academic Affairs at Ohio State University 1994, 1). If there is dissonance between departmental practices during a search and the institution's professed commitments to diversifying the faculty, the fault line will be evident.

Responsibility for diversifying the faculty lies with people at many levels in an academic institution. Therefore, it is essential to align departmental and institutional commitments to faculty diversity by establishing measurable departmental goals. When these goals are met, top-level administrators should acknowledge the achievement publicly as a way of indicating that the institution is serious about its commitment to diversity. For example, since academic departments are both producers and consumers of potential faculty, the number of doctoral and master's students of color accepted and graduated from specific programs should be used to assess the degree to which each department is contributing to the institutional goal of diversifying the faculty.

In addition, some institutions create strong incentives to promote faculty diversity through the overall faculty reward structure. In other words, departments that are successfully recruiting candidates for vacancies and retaining faculty of color by offering mentoring, professional development, and research opportunities are recognized and rewarded. Virginia Tech, for example, has established an exemplary department awards program. Three departments are selected annually for excellence in relation to the announced theme. Selected departments receive a significant cash award, recognition at an elaborate reception, and permission to note the award on departmental letterhead for a five-year period. Recent themes for the program centered on diversifying the faculty, staff, and/or student body, and infusing multicultural perspectives in teaching, research, and/or outreach programs. Some scholars also recommend making links for department heads between merit pay and diversifying the faculty (Knowles and Harleston 1994; Makay 1990; Sullivan and Nowlin 1990; Wilson 1994).

3. Creating a Welcoming Environment

If a search committee's work is ultimately to succeed in terms of the retention and further recruitment of faculty of color, the institution must be ready to welcome diversity. The results of a study conducted by Turner and Myers (2000) reveal that, while the reasons faculty of color leave positions vary, a hostile campus environment would certainly be cause for a quick retreat. It may also discourage other potential applicants from seriously considering employment at such an institution. By contrast, an institution that provides an environment supportive of faculty of color is attractive and thus facilitates recruitment and retention.

An excellent way to assess how welcoming your campus environment is to faculty of color is to conduct a cultural audit. Designed to reveal how different groups perceive the overall environment, cultural audits are usually done through surveys of faculty, students, or staff. These audits can illuminate specific problem areas on campus, reveal whether some groups are subjected to hostile environments, and measure progress over time. Examples of cultural audits can be found on DiversityWeb (www.diversityweb.org) and in *Assessing Campus Diversity Initiatives* (García et al. 2002).

There are other institutional markers that indicate whether a college is likely to be perceived as welcoming by faculty of color. Institutional leaders, for instance, might consider the following sorts of questions:

- Does our mission statement clearly articulate the educational value and societal obligations of diversity?
- Do we have a vibrant ethnic studies program, a well-thought-out diversity requirement, and multiple opportunities for students to be introduced to diversity throughout the curriculum?
- Does our campus have research centers that focus on issues of race?
- How structurally diverse is our faculty, staff, and student body? What is the

retention rate for people of color in these various groups? What is the tenure rate? Do we have people of color serving in leadership positions?

- Do we offer college-wide academic, cultural, and other events that include people of color as speakers and key participants?
- Have there been racial incidents on campus recently, and if so, how have we handled them?
- How do our residential programs take advantage of the diversity within the student body?
- Is there evidence that our institution has made steady progress in addressing diversity issues over time?
- What is the nature of our relationship to our local communities of color nearby? Do we have a history of partnerships with these communities?

In order to successfully recruit and retain faculty of color, colleges and universities must take proactive steps to create a welcoming environment by infusing diversity initiatives into a variety of areas—mission statements, senior administration, academic affairs, and student affairs. Model institutions also can point to a substantial history of multiple kinds of partnerships with local communities of color, thereby offering new faculty a variety of ways to connect easily with these communities. Individual departments can also contribute to the overall campus environment. As Johnsrud and Heck (1994) note, an academic department can take deliberate efforts to foster collaboration, collegiality, and intellectual cross-fertilization. Departments that value diversity are marked by mutual respect and supportive behavior, which are

often demonstrated by such practices as collaborative research and mentoring initiatives for junior faculty. Such a departmental climate would be a major attraction to any faculty member.

Finally, it is worth noting that even the smallest of details can be an important part of the total picture. Was the letter of application acknowledged? Was it acknowledged in a timely way? Did one or more committee members call in anticipation of or as a follow-up to the interview to see if they could answer any more questions? Had the committee anticipated ahead of time what might be particular concerns for faculty of color on their campus (i.e., housing concerns, schooling options for children, access to communities of color on and off campus)? The small details can speak volumes to candidates, but especially to candidates of color assessing how welcoming a climate may be.

4. Securing Resources

Once an institution commits itself to diversifying its faculty, securing the necessary resources becomes essential to the ultimate success of a search committee. Most of these resources are typically provided in any good search. However, additional resources can be provided to recruit, support, and retain faculty of color. A faculty development survey of 486 colleges and universities in the Midwest found that high minority faculty development budgets and increased funding for minority recruitment have a direct correlation to positive effects on minority hiring rates (Turner and Myers 2000). Many institutions, for example, cover professional travel expenses, provide funds for moving, or help in securing spousal employment. Departments can also subsidize and/or support professional development and research activities as incentives in the recruiting process.

Rather than waiting for a vacancy to occur, some institutions create funding pools from which departments can draw to hire qualified minority scholars when an opportunity presents itself. These funding pools, often called Target of Opportunity Appointments, are leveraged against future vacancies, new positions, or are provided as additional faculty lines. Many institutions are now creating faculty fellows programs to hire post-docs or ABD ("all but the dissertation") graduate students as faculty. This type of grow-your-own program for minority faculty development promotes the identification and recruitment of potential faculty of color, sometimes from outside of academe.

One major midwestern research university enters into a contract with prospective faculty that requires the individual to complete his or her doctorate while teaching two sections of the same course. Each participant receives tuition remission to their home school, an office, a travel allowance, equipment resources, and fringe benefits on the basis of 0.75 FTE (full-time equivalent) faculty member. Upon completion of the degree, the positions are guaranteed for conversion to tenure track and the salary is automatically changed from 0.75 to 1.00 FTE. There is also the option to negotiate salary when converting to full time status, and there are no strings attached concerning the number of years the individual must agree to remain employed at the university. At this midwestern university, the program recently exceeded its minimum goal of three minority faculty hires

converted to tenure track (Turner and Myers 2000). The success of this program has resulted in its expansion to other departments at the university.

Although many faculty of color hired in such programs praise the efforts, they also report being treated as "second class citizens" by some peers who view them as illegitimate because they did not enter the academic ranks

Since one of the most important tasks of the search committee is to expand the pool of qualified applicants, new and diverse networks must be developed to counter the persistence of segregated networks.

through "regular" pathways. It is worth pointing out that the regular pathways have always included innovative processes for hiring faculty with particular talents deemed essential to the academic enterprise.

5. Countering Segregated Networks

In the lives of busy professionals, information shared as part of regular contact and communication can determine who finds out about a position opening in time to prepare a competitive application. These networks often help to identify and actively recruit promising candidates. Too often, people of color are overlooked because they are not part of the primary networks of senior faculty and administrators. Since one of the most important tasks of the search committee is to expand the pool of qualified applicants, new and diverse networks must be developed to counter the persistence of segregated networks.

In order to yield a candidate pool that is as diverse as possible, departments and institutions should consciously develop external networks within which to circulate position announcements. A good way to begin is to establish contact with faculty of color on campus or at a neighboring college or with professionals in the local community. Then, once a faculty position opens, nominations can be sought from these contacts. For example, departments can develop and maintain ties to relevant doctoral-granting institutions and department chairs on neighboring campuses. In addition to providing updates on potential candidates, these individuals can give insight into the employment trends of their minority students to help the hiring institution adjust to marketplace changes. Several liberal arts colleges, especially those with limited fiscal resources, have developed an inter-institutional consortia to effectively pool resources on potential candidates. For example, Swarthmore College, Bryn Mawr College, and Haverford College, all within a thirty minute drive of each other, have hired a single person with joint appointments at all three institutions.

Another useful way to develop new networks is to establish and maintain contacts among minority interest groups affiliated with national educational and disciplinary associations. Relationships with the chairs or representatives of such groups should be established so that regular communication eventually becomes a natural and institutionalized part of campus interactions. Thus a functioning and robust multi-racial

network is already in place when faculty openings occur.

The Compact for Faculty Diversity (www.wiche.edu/ DocScholars/compact.htm), for example, creates programs that foster a community of established faculty of color and their peers to support students of color as they complete their degrees and enter the profession. Other initiatives support potential faculty from specific racial and ethnic groups within specific disciplines. The Hispanic Theological Initiative (www.htiptogram.org), for example, provides support to Hispanic scholars interested in faculty positions at theological schools and seminaries. Departments with established links to programs like these are more likely to attract candidates of color.

National associations are also great resources. The Association of American Colleges & Universities (www.aacu-edu.org), especially through its Office of Diversity, Equity, and Global Initiatives, can help link search committees to AAC&U's broad national network of faculty and administrators of color. The American Association of University Professors (www.aaup.org) Committee on Historically Black Institutions and the Status of Minorities in the Profession is a potentially useful resource for search committees. The same is true of the American Educational Research Association (www.aera.net) Committee on the Role and Status of Minorities in Educational Research and Development and the several Special Interest Groups which focus on issues relevant to racial and ethnic minority groups. The American Psychological Association (www.apa.org) has a Commission on Ethnic Minority Recruitment, Retention, and Training in Psychology. All such groups cannot be listed here, but faculty in each department need to be aware of the relevant associations with which to maintain contact.

Departments and institutions can also make and sustain connections with colleges and universities that educate a greater number of graduate students of color. Lists of all Hispanic Serving Institutions (www.ed.gov /offices/OIIA/Hispanic/hsi/hsi9798/hsitable.html), Historically Black Colleges and Universities (eric-web.tc.columbia.edu/hbcu/gowebs.html), and Tribal Colleges (www.aihec.org/college.htm) are readily available and can be provided to search committees. In addition, some predominantly white research institutions also award a sizeable number of graduate degrees to students of color (see Appendix B). It is important to identify these institutions so that colleagues and department heads from the relevant discipline can be incorporated into institutional or departmental networks. Personal contact can then be made to encourage nominations.

The Preparing Future Faculty (PFF) program (www.preparing-faculty.org) is another good recruitment resource. Sponsored by the Association of American Colleges and Universities and the Council of Graduate Schools, PFF encourages institutions to re-think and reorganize the preparation of doctoral students who aspire to become faculty. Schools participating in PFF programs ask faculty to bring their intellectual and experiential knowledge to the professional development of the next generation of academics. Through PFF, graduate students are prepared for the kinds of responsibilities they will encounter as faculty members at a variety of institutions. PFF graduates of color would be excellent additions to any candidate pool.

In addition, Wolf-Wendel (1995) provides a list of baccalaureate institutions that produce large numbers of African–American women and Latinas who go on to pursue doctoral degrees (see Appendix C). While these programs and institutions may not yield candidates for today's searches, they may yield future candidates by enabling the campus to establish a relationship either with the program officials or with participants.

The Search Process

Search committees often approach their charge in a passive, routine way: advertise the position in publications (e.g., *The Chronicle of Higher Education, Black Issues in Higher Education, The Hispanic Outlook in Higher Education*), evaluate resumes, invite three to five candidates for campus interviews, and then make an offer. To redress the current underrepresentation of faculty of color, however, search committees must take a more proactive approach and genuinely *search* for candidates of color. The search process is not just important for recruiting faculty of color for a specific position. All steps taken during the search process can contribute to a solid foundation for the successful retention of faculty of color hired as well as to successful recruitment in the future. In suggesting strategies for enhancing the likelihood of a successful search for faculty of color, this chapter is focused on eight steps:

- Forming the search committee
- Educating the search committee on personnel issues
- Debunking the myths
- Creating the position description
- Attracting a diverse candidate pool
- Examining hiring biases
- Hosting the campus visit
- Making the offer

1. Forming the Search Committee

When a faculty vacancy occurs, the department chair usually appoints several faculty members to a search committee. At the onset of the committee's work, its charge, specific functions, and the extent of its authority should be clearly defined. For a successful search, diversifying the faculty must be strongly articulated as a top priority when the committee receives its charge.

All steps taken during the search process can contribute to a solid foundation for the successful retention of faculty of color hired as well as to successful recruitment in the future.

The composition of the search committee is critical to its success. By involving people with different points of view or by bringing in a fresh face, the chair can ensure that multiple perspectives and fresh ideas are brought to bear in evaluating candidates. Also, people of color, whether administrators or faculty, should have a presence on the committee. One scholar of color, an endowed professor, emphasizes the importance of a diverse search committee. "Be sure that there are respected and highly visible people of color [who are committed to hiring of minorities] on the committee….This sends an important signal to the larger community that the search is a serious search. Highly visible and respected persons of color should be consulted about the composition of the committee and about the strategy." Of course, it is clear that faculty of color, as other faculty, may differ in their views of the qualification of candidates.

Efforts to diversify the faculty continue to be among the least successful elements of campus commitments to diversity.

When selecting search committee members, chairs must be cautious of the dynamics that can occur when assistant professors of color are placed on search committees along with tenured majority faculty. On the one hand, diverse representation on the committee is vitally important. On the other hand, junior faculty may be placed in an untenable position if, in order to champion their candidate, they must challenge the thinking of senior professors and administrators who will one day vote on their tenure.

To meet their commitment to constructing diverse search committees, many colleges and universities with low numbers of faculty of color have invited doctoral graduates of color and scholars of color from neighboring institutions or disciplinary associations to join their search committees. In many cases, reaching out to these colleagues also yields longer-term benefits in graduate student recruitment, intern and job placement, and research collaborations.

2. Educating the Search Committee on Personnel Issues

Although search committees most often contain senior scholars, it should not be assumed that members are equally competent about personnel matters or that they have common views about diversity and equity issues. Therefore, education is a necessary component of an effective search. This process also can be used to create a common bond and a spirit of collaboration among committee members. As a starting place, all search committees should be informed about affirmative action policies and institutional hiring protocols.

Institutions must adhere to federal mandates requiring search committees to make a good faith effort to develop an inclusive applicant pool and to assure the implementation of individual campus affirmative action policies and practices[3]. Because so much erroneous information exists about affirmative action, search committees should be given national and campus-specific facts about the rationale, implementation, and effects of the policy. For instance, despite affirmative action and institutional efforts to diversify faculty, people of color remain severely underrepresented in the profession. Efforts to diversify the faculty continue to be among the least successful elements of campus commitments to diversity. Most campuses have been unsuccessful in their attempts to attract and retain faculty of color, thereby maintaining their largely white, male composition (Smith, Wolf, and Busenberg 1996; Sullivan and Nowlin 1990; Turner and Myers 2000; Harvey 2001). To guard against misinformation and behaviors associated with it, a search committee should tap the expertise of campus affirmative action officials at the onset of its work and, in some instances, at several points during the search and selection process.

Search committees are often unaware of how to carry out their duties effectively within legal boundaries. Jonathan Alger (1999), former counsel for the American Association of University Professors and now assistant general counsel for the University of Michigan, argues that institutions must work with their legal counsel to demonstrate that there is alignment between legal standards and what campuses are doing. He underscores that the Supreme Court decision in the 1978 *Bakke* case is still the law of the land, with regard to students in particular. In this case, the Court held that race could be considered as one among a number of other factors that contributes to the education of students, and that student diversity in higher education is a compelling state interest (*Regents of the University of California v. Bakke* 1978). With the many legal challenges to affirmative action, state referenda, and institutional policies that have an impact on the hiring process, search committees should be sure to know what applies to their institution.

While the *Bakke* decision specifically supports the use of race as a factor in student admission, at least one state court has connected the goals of a racially diverse faculty as analogous to the goal of a diverse student body (*Farmer v. University and Community College System of Nevada* 1998). Furthermore, Qualiana and Finkelstein (2000) discuss the Supreme Court decisions and Equal Employment Opportunity Commission rules which provide a series of steps and examples that support programs continuing to strive for diverse faculty representation in academe. In spite of current challenges to affirmative action, the authors do not suggest that efforts to attain diversity among faculty be discontinued. However, in addition to implementing employment criteria that may lead indirectly to racial diversity, Qualiana and Finkelstein urge that "institutions review their plans not only for legality but for effectiveness, and revise the plans accordingly" (17).

Search committees should develop a protocol to ensure fairness and consistency in the search process, if standards do not already exist. The protocol will help guide the committee in searching for applicants, initially screening applicants to form a short list, interviewing the final candidates, and selecting the final candidates to recommend to the dean. The protocol must ensure that all policies, laws, and procedures are followed to provide fairness and consistency in the process. A rationale for candidates selected for the short list will need to be submitted to the campus personnel and affirmative action offices. If the committee is unfamiliar with the process of developing such hiring protocols, training should be provided and information on strategies to recruit a diverse pool of candidates should be emphasized.

In essence, all colleges and universities have the freedom to select their faculty. But in adhering to legal regulation, it is important to examine these policies and practices at each stage of the hiring process. Everything legally possible should be done to ensure that the pool of candidates is racially and ethnically diverse.

3. Debunking the Myths

Various myths and stereotypes about minorities in academe can inadvertently impede progress in hiring faculty of color. Some are focused on the institution: "our institution cannot compete for doctorates of color because everyone wants them" or "we cannot match the high salaries offered to faculty of color." Others are focused on prospective candidates: "there are no qualified candidates of color for our open faculty positions;" "faculty of color would not want to come to our campus;" or "faculty of color will leave for more money and prestige." Still others appeal more directly to racism: "recruiting faculty color takes away opportunities for white faculty." Such myths and stereotypes can have an insidious effect on the search committee process and should be addressed as part of preparing search committee members for their work.

According to Sullivan and Nowlin (1990), five prevalent myths hinder the hiring process: good minority faculty go to the best universities; espousing Equal Employment Opportunity (EEO) doctrine is enough; to hire minorities, standards must be lowered; minorities will not go to predominantly white institutions; and minorities prefer the private sector. Swoboda (1993) identifies these same myths as perhaps the most difficult to dispel because they are most often invoked to veil deeply held beliefs of ethnic or gender inferiority. These beliefs produce a type of negative mindset that becomes a self-fulfilling prophecy. This negative mindset assumes that the institution and department are completely rational and unbiased in their decision-making and that cultural, racial, ethnic, and gender biases are simply nonexistent. As a consequence, when these assumptions of neutrality underlie screening and evaluation processes, there is grave danger that minority and female candidates will be rejected. Such rejection is often attributed to the candidate's lack of qualifications or interest, rather than to the

prejudice that is present and that influences the process.

In *Achieving Faculty Diversity* (1996), Smith, Wolf, and Busenberg present research that disputes many myths. Their examination of the employment experiences of 393 white and minority men and women with Ph.D.s who were recipients of prestigious Ford, Mellon, and Spencer doctoral fellowships, for example, found that the assertions that faculty of color are in great demand and subject to bidding wars are overly exaggerated. In fact, only 11 percent of scholars of color were actively sought after by several institutions simultaneously—which means that 89 percent were not subject to competitive bidding wars. Smith also found that many faculty of color, even those in the sciences, are, in fact, under-employed. Moreover, in an investigation of faculty turnover, Turner and Myers (2000) found that faculty of color do not shift jobs faster than whites. While minority faculty may leave their institutions at rates similar to those of their white counterparts, they are not being hired at the same rate as white faculty. Therefore, the turnover may appear larger, but in reality it is not.

A final category of myth worth mentioning is known as the "model minority myth," according to which certain populations are perceived as so successful that they do not experience discrimination. In some areas, for example, the success rates for Asian Pacific Americans (APAs) are impressively high. Yet APAs are still subject to racial discrimination. In *Confronting the Myths* (1996), Cho identifies several "beyond parity" types of discrimination faced by APA faculty. Specifically discussed are the denial of tenure and promotion;

professional and disciplinary tracking; the absence of APAs at the executive and managerial levels in higher education; sexual and racial harassment; accent discrimination; and methods of counting foreign nationals in campus affirmative action reports which inflate APA numbers.

Myths and stereotypes about minorities in academe must be addressed consistently. One effective way to do so is for campus leaders to create and support discussion arenas related to institutional diversity goals. Deans, department chairs, and senior faculty should establish direct contact with faculty from racial and ethnic groups other than their own in these arenas with the goal of better understanding how myths and stereotypes are manifested in their campus context. Research demonstrates that the development of sustained, personal relationships can help to dispel racial myths and stereotypes (Allport 1954). Studies by Duster (1991) and antonio (2001) show that social distance allows individuals to maintain their stereotypes of each other. Campus leaders should also sponsor professional and communal activities to provide opportunities for positive inter- and intra-racial interaction, to help build a shared sense of purpose, and to promote networking among all faculty.

4. Creating the Position Description

Whenever a vacancy occurs—whether for an existing position or for a newly created position, search committees should carefully review the position description to ensure that it is aligned with the commitment to diversify the faculty. Search committees must guard against writing or recycling a position description that will automatically "define out" candidates of color.

The following are suggestions for creating a position description most likely to yield a wide and inclusive candidate pool:

- Make sure the announcement strongly expresses the university's commitment to affirmative action/equal opportunity and encourages minorities to apply.
- Develop broad descriptions of scholarship, experience, and disciplinary background; take into consideration the specific needs of the department as well as the broad needs of the institution.
- Where appropriate, label qualifications *preferred* instead of *required*; use *should* instead of *must*.
- Whenever possible, be flexible with arbitrary numeric measures, such as years of experience.
- In addition to a letter of application and a curriculum vitae, request other materials such as copies of articles, letters of reference, and samples of course syllabi.
- Ask applicants to describe their experience with diversity issues, diverse students, and working in multicultural environments.

Attention must also be paid to the language used in a position description. Phrases like those listed below can ensure that the strengths of some minority applicants are not overlooked.

- Experience with a variety of teaching methods and/or curricular perspectives
- Previous experience interacting with communities of color
- Experience in cultures other than their own
- Academic experiences and interests in culturally diverse groups
- Interest in developing and implementing curricula that address multicultural issues

- Demonstrated success in working with diverse populations of students

5. Attracting a Diverse Candidate Pool

Search committees must do more than simply issue a job announcement and wait to receive vita. Ultimately, getting the right person requires active recruitment of a broad range of candidates. Developing and aggressively implementing a comprehensive recruitment

Developing and aggressively implementing a comprehensive recruitment plan that uses multiple recruitment strategies simultaneously will significantly increase the diversity of the applicant pool.

plan that uses multiple recruitment strategies simultaneously will significantly increase the diversity of the applicant pool. At this phase of the search process, campuses that have successfully established ties with various communities of color (see pages 6–8), can access those networks, circulate the job announcement, and solicit applications and nominations.

In addition, position openings should be advertised through programs such as the National Name Exchange Program (www.grad.washington.edu/nameexch/national/), a consortium of twenty-seven nationally known universities which annually collect and exchange the names of talented minority students. Advertisements should also

target minority graduate students through pipeline projects, which can be found at a variety of institutions and disciplinary associations, and through undergraduate research programs, such as the Mellon Minority Undergraduate Fellowship Program (www.mellon.org/awmf.html), the Howard Hughes Undergraduate Biological Sciences Program (www.hhmi.org/grants/undergraduate), and the Bill and Melinda Gates Millennium Scholars Program (www.gmsp.org/main.cfm). It is also important to advertise in journals and periodicals that reach graduate students and faculty of color.

In addition to advertising a specific faculty position, search committees should make a conscious effort to market the campus itself as welcoming to prospective faculty of color. "In order to attract eligible minorities," one long-time university administrator with broad experience in marketing recommends "an extensive and comprehensive public relations' campaign to publicize how [your campus] might be attractive to the scholarly or collegial endeavors in which those eligible minorities are likely to be involved." In other words, it is not enough simply to create a welcoming environment, as described in part one; prospective applicants must be made aware of it.

Catalogues and prospectuses are excellent tools for marketing campuses to prospective students. Yet, in most cases, no parallel documents are available to prospective faculty. Publishing a viewbook or campus guide that articulates your campus as welcoming to faculty of color would be an excellent way to market the campus and to encourage a diverse applicant pool. Such a publication, formal or informal, could address common issues raised by faculty ranging from research opportunities, computer facilities, and sites for collegiality (organized by research and teaching units), to housing and relevant local community interests. Information reflecting an institutional commitment to diversity could also be included. Moreover, the process of developing the faculty viewbook or campus guide could itself become an arena for interdepartmental faculty dialogue on the institution's diversity goals.

The conduct of job searches has been transformed by technology, which offers many opportunities for rethinking the way advertisements and job descriptions are constructed. For example, the job advertisement no longer needs to cover everything about the institution or position. Instead, a brief advertisement can include a link to the full job description posted on the departmental or university Web site. The full job description should provide prospective applicants with sufficient information both to determine whether the position is an appropriate fit and to prepare a more informative cover letter. This use of technology keeps advertising costs to a minimum and provides even more information to candidates. The Web page on which the position description is posted can also include links to various university resources—cultural centers, women's centers, family/community information, related research centers on campus, a statement of commitment by senior administrators concerning diversity hiring, etc.

Typically, the provost's office becomes aware of candidates only after a "short list" has been decided upon at the departmental level. A large research university in the West has adopted a very promising and innovative use of technology to enable the provost's office to monitor the applicant pool as it develops. A newly established faculty equity office has created a Web page for all faculty searches, and applicants can file applications online. If a search is not attracting enough minority applicants, questions can be raised early and the provost's office can keep the search open until the pool is adequately diverse.

While formal searching techniques are helpful in initiating contact with prospective applicants, personal outreach to candidates is sometimes needed.

The following anecdote from an academic administrator demonstrates that, even if a committee does everything right in advertising both the position and the campus, success is not guaranteed by formal methods alone.

We just completed several faculty searches. All of the individuals we selected are faculty of color. How did we make this happen? We ran the search out of the dean's office where there was strong commitment to hire faculty of color; we announced the positions as furthering the school's urban mission,...the language signaled our commitments and interests. However, none of the candidates actually applied for the position. We found them and we went after them very aggressively. We also made our interest in them very clear. We gave them the royal treatment on their visits here. I doubt we would have achieved this if we would have waited for applicants. Going after specific individuals requires that at least one person in the search committee has the contacts to identify individuals.

While formal searching techniques are helpful in initiating contact with prospective applicants, personal outreach to candidates is sometimes needed. The examples listed below send a message that an institution is committed to increasing the representation of people of color among its faculty.

- Make telephone calls.
- Send personalized letters to potential applicants or to those who might refer potential applicants.
- Write e-mails.
- Talk face-to-face with people who might nominate potential candidates, stressing the institution's commitment to diversity.
- Approach potential applicants at professional meetings, and personally encourage their application for the position.
- Consult with minority faculty members on campus about the types of outreach they consider most effective.

These efforts must demonstrate genuine interest in the specific candidate being recruited. For instance, a letter sent to a potential candidate must demonstrate the writer's knowledge of this person's scholarly expertise and explain the types of contributions they could make to the program if they were to be hired. At best, a general form letter can make a neutral impression or, at worst, a very negative impression.

Successful search committees combine their recruitment efforts by not merely relying on targeted mailings, but accompanying those efforts with personal networking. Networking should be a personal and ongoing effort. If resources are extremely limited, telephone and personal contacts will generally yield better results than mass mailings.

6. Examining Hiring Biases

The initial screening stage of the search committee process typically results in a short list of candidates from which the most promising are selected for an interview. At this stage, it is critical to consider expanding the evaluation criteria. Ultimately, to diversify the faculty, the criteria used for hiring and promotion must also be diversified.

A major barrier to diversifying the faculty is the tendency of many search committees and final hiring authorities (chairs and deans) to look for faculty who are "just like us" (Light 1994). Estela Bensimon (2000) identifies this phenomenon as an example of "dysconscious racism," a term coined by Joyce E. King (1991) to describe her students' "limited and distorted understandings" about inequity and cultural diversity. King believes that such misrepresentations of equity can hinder or subvert equitable actions. Bensimon applies this theory to the experiences of faculty of color in higher education institutions. She writes:

Examples of dysconscious racism include the predisposition of search committees to look for and favor candidates who are like themselves, not necessarily racially or ethnically, but in terms of educational background, social skills, values, and behaviors, and to reject candidates whose education, experience, or research interests deviate from the traditional academic mold.

One might say that search committees, without intending to, look for "Afro-Saxons" or "Hispanic-Saxons."

Marchese and Lawrence (1998) refer to this practice as "sectorism" and suggest that focusing on the abilities of the candidates and on the criteria optimal for the job are keys to avoiding it. According to Smith, Wolf, and Busenberg (1996), a lack of diversity on a search committee limits the potential for introducing new perspectives to the process of evaluation. Smith's conclusion is reiterated by Bensimon, Ward, and Saunders (2000), who state that a department or a search committee made up of individuals with similar backgrounds and experience may lack sufficient creativity to think of innovative strategies for successfully attracting candidates of color. Difference is not likely to be sought or nurtured in such situations.

Another bias in hiring practices was uncovered by a study of how black candidates fared in searches (Mickelson and Oliver 1991). The study found that potential faculty candidates are most often eliminated on the basis of their graduate school and that the highest rankings tend to go to candidates from the most elite doctoral-granting universities. The study strongly suggests that search committees assume that only candidates holding degrees from top graduate programs are worthy of consideration. As Mickelson and Oliver point out, scholars of color may take different routes to the professoriat than majority scholars. Colleges and universities should recruit candidates who have distinguished themselves in business, industry, community agencies, government, and military settings as well as in traditional educational settings. In addition, search committees should look beyond publishing records alone to other measures of academic merit. Teaching excellence, work experience—including non-academic work, service, and outreach records should also be considered when evaluating candidates for a faculty position.

7. Hosting the Campus Visit

The campus visit provides candidates with an opportunity to showcase their academic pursuits and interests. And, because candidates are evaluating the campus even as they are being evaluated, it also provides an opportunity to highlight an institution's strengths. Because of this dual purpose, the campus visit can be an extremely important part of the effort to diversify the faculty.

Whenever possible, candidates should be provided with the itinerary for the visit in advance. They also should be made aware of the kind of presentation they will be expected to make and of the audience for it. And, if raised by the candidate, the interests and needs of the candidate's family or partner should be addressed during the interview. The search committee can also help the candidate identify professional networks on campus. For example, the committee can provide opportunities, during the visit, for the candidate to consult with faculty and students of color from other departments. Of course, since networks should not be limited by race or ethnicity, the committee should also schedule meetings with majority faculty who have similar scholarly interests. These kinds of meetings are especially useful when there is a small number of faculty of color in the field or discipline of the potential hire. Genuine interest in the candidate is clearly demonstrated when committee members are conversant with the candidate's publications and other work.

During the campus visit, interactions with the candidate must present the campus realistically. At the outset, it is also very important to make clear to candidates any unique aspects or unwritten expectations of the position. This is part of maintaining clear and open communications. Presenting the campus realistically includes admitting problems and weaknesses as well as highlighting areas of strength and support. The committee should ensure that the department and faculty relations are represented accurately. Departmental expectations regarding teaching, research, service, and the promotion processes should be communicated honestly. The search committee should also discuss information on tenure procedures and the level of departmental support the candidate should anticipate. If a candidate accepts the position in the absence of such thorough and straightforward discussions, the new hire is left to learn by trial and error, which may increase the chances for dissatisfaction, isolation from department activities, distance from colleagues, lower productivity, and eventual departure.

A well-hosted campus visit allows candidates to make well-informed decisions on whether the position and the place is a right "fit" for them. This process also enables the search committee to broaden its evaluation of the candidate. Evaluation forms should be provided to all parties involved in the campus visit, and the responses should be included in the discussions to select the final candidate. Asking respondents to comment on the process will also provide the institution with information about how to improve subsequent campus visits.

8. Making the Offer

Negotiating the compensation package is without a doubt the most important part of making the offer. These negotiations must be handled carefully; a poorly made offer can easily jeopardize the seeds of retention sown over the course of the entire search process.

Because the dean or committee chair already has a salary cap in mind when making the offer, the onus of guessing that magical figure is placed on the candidate. This kind of guessing game can be counterproductive. Since salary information is often public, particularly for state institutions, prospective faculty may already have a good idea of the salary range. If the offer is not in keeping with the salary range for the expertise and experience of the candidate, he or she may find the offer insulting. On the other hand, some potential candidates may be novices at negotiating salary. If a novice accepts a position at a salary that is not in keeping with the standard, then the discrepancy may be viewed as an inexcusable betrayal when it is discovered. This may affect the productivity of the faculty member and make him or her more receptive to offers made by other institutions.

Although salary is a major enticement or deterrent, the conversation regarding the compensation package should include other incentives the institution is willing to provide. Hiring officials should consider broadening the package to include intangibles, like reduced teaching loads, professional development, and research support. These opportunities should be discussed during the visit when possible. Of course, expenses incurred by the candidate in pursuit of the position should be fully compensated whenever possible.

After the Search

The successful recruitment of faculty of color is only half the battle. Campuses will not achieve the desired effect of a racially and ethnically diverse faculty unless the faculty hired decide to stay. To retain faculty and to reap the benefits of their diversity, campus leaders must work to ensure a collegial and intellectually stimulating environment for new hires. This chapter discusses two crucial ways to promote faculty retention:

- Support of the new hire
- Assessment of the search process and outcome

It is vitally important for search committees to think about retention. Committee members are well positioned to anticipate the potential challenges faced by newly hired faculty of color and to participate as campus leaders in shaping the post-hire climate for faculty of color.

1. Supporting the New Hire

All faculty face significant pressure to excel at teaching and scholarship. Yet faculty of color at predominantly white institutions or in predominately white departments may face additional pressures as well. These include emotional stresses, such as feelings of exclusion, isolation, alienation, and devaluation as well as increased demands on the time given to campus service. These pressures can result in an uncomfortable work environment that undermines the productivity and satisfaction of faculty of color. It may even discourage their entry into academic life entirely.

Turner and Myers (2000) conducted a study to learn more about the workplace perceptions of faculty of color in midwestern college and university settings. They found that, whether in a tenured or tenure-track position, most faculty of color cited firsthand experiences of racial and ethnic bias and intimidation in the workplace. Study participants identified the following as major concerns:

■ Being denied tenure or promotion due to race/ethnicity

Faculty respondents perceive that they did not fit the profile for promotion. Other studies have described the heightened tensions associated with achieving tenure for faculty who must confront discrimination linked to racist and other prejudices.

■ Being expected to work harder than white colleagues

In order to be equal to whites in academe, faculty of color perceive that higher performance is expected from them than from their white colleagues. If they are perceived to fail in any situation, such failures are generalized to all others of their race or ethnic background.

■ Having color/ethnicity given more attention than credentials

Faculty of color report that their race or ethnic background is among the first things mentioned as they are introduced on campus, not their academic credentials or accomplishments. Many report feeling diminished in their professional capacities, with their difference equated with inferiority.

■ Being treated as a token

Study respondents reported that they are seen as mere concessions to affirmative action or diversity requirements. They do not truly have an equal voice to influence their department or campus culture.

■ Lacking support or validation for research on minority issues

Many faculty of color report that their research, especially if it focuses on racial and ethnic concerns, is devalued in hiring, tenure, and promotion processes.

■ Being expected to handle minority affairs

Faculty of color report that they are expected to be experts in addressing any campus issues related to their racial or ethnic group. This is not expected of most white faculty.

■ Having too few minorities on campus

In addition to feelings of isolation expressed by faculty of color, their small numbers perpetuate the myth that minorities cannot achieve in academe.

The sensitivity of campus leadership to the above listed quality of life work issues coupled with the implementation of policies and practices to address these concerns are major factors contributing to the retention of faculty of color.

Faculty hiring should be viewed as a long-term investment rather than as a short-term fix to gain numerical advantage. The department and institution should be committed to their new hire's scholarly growth. Leave nothing to chance. Regular follow-up after hiring a new faculty member is essential; it helps ease the transition and may uncover as well as address issues that often develop in the first few months in the position. Simple things, such as having an office ready for a new faculty member, can help to set a welcoming tone. One academic administrator says that her institution provides a welcome basket for new junior faculty, which may include paid subscriptions to journals related to their area of interest and recent texts as well as other publications on teaching approaches. In addition, all conditions in the final letter of agreement must be upheld. Although there is a legal rationale, there are also emotional reasons for campuses to ensure that all pre-employment agreements are in place upon the arrival of new faculty.

During the transition phase, continued contact with the new hire is crucial in order to discover and address any misunderstandings or dissatisfactions. At this stage, campus administrators and faculty must listen to the issues raised and avoid becoming defensive. They must understand the stress that major life changes, such as moving and changing positions, has on any new hire. In many instances, for faculty of color, this is coupled with a transition to a new campus environment and community with few, if any, faculty, staff, or students who share their racial or ethnic background.

However, as noted by an academic administrator whose institution has not retained many faculty of color, retention goes beyond the transition and start up phase.

> While the loss of minority faculty to other institutions can be attributed to poor start-up packages and less than competitive salaries, the powerful inducements to leave stem from dissatisfaction and problems encountered once [the faculty member is] in place. The development of collegial networks and [rewards] for service responsibilities are the best [strategies for retaining faculty of color]. The University must begin to move in the direction of developing a more positive reputation for its commitment to diversity.

Another retention problem is caused by the unspoken expectation of service demands, particularly those activities that carry little weight in periodic tenure reviews. When there are few faculty members of color on campus, those present are often asked to serve on numerous departmental, college, or university-wide committees. For similar reasons, community groups also draw on these same faculty to represent the campus on agency committees, government boards, and other service groups. Although the efforts of these entities to achieve diverse representation is commendable, campus officials should be mindful of the extraordinary burden such invitations place on faculty of color. At the very least, campus officials should make clear to faculty of color the relative weight of such service so the individual faculty member can make an informed decision about his or her involvement. At the very most, such service should be equally valued and rewarded in the promotion and tenure process.

Also, professors of color often become official or unofficial advisers for minority students and organizations on campus. Because many have a strong commitment to help sustain a diverse campus environment, to provide community service, and to assist students of color, they are often reluctant to decline such offers. The overload often results in stress and may contribute to many people of color leaving the professoriat.

■ Critical Mass

Perhaps the most important way to retain professors of color is to create a diverse faculty. Without a critical mass of people of color as colleagues, faculty of color often feel isolated and alienated and are likely to leave. Therefore, if your recruiting stops with hiring one person of color or with just a few, you may be caught in a repeating cycle of hiring one person then losing that person, then hiring another person.

Wheaton College, a small liberal arts college in New England, made headlines by hiring several Black scholars. As Wheaton's President Dale R. Marshall explains, the college undertook an aggressive recruitment approach.

Wheaton recruited aggressively but took the same sorts of steps that all colleges do in the pursuit of hot prospects, black or white. This approach included multiple hires of minority faculty; campus leadership paving the way by granting departments autonomy and power to make decisions quickly; financial and other incentives to make positions more attractive;

and taking the initiative to identify, contact, and recruit talented faculty of color at professional organization meetings and elsewhere (Krebs 2000, 53).

When asked, Wheaton's faculty pointed to hiring more than one minority faculty (referred to as cluster hiring) as one of the best retention strategies. This lessens the sense of isolation and tokenism that often makes the new hire feel devalued.

■ Mentoring

The importance of mentoring has long been recognized, but minority professors often have fewer mentoring opportunities than their majority counterparts. Many faculty of color confront special obstacles, ranging from racism among their students to feelings of isolation within their departments. Because of the chilly reception that faculty of color often receive, they may have a greater need for mentors more often than their white counterparts. Thus, the absence of mentoring opportunities is particularly detrimental. Unfortunately, many departments do not have senior minority faculty members, and many minority professors feel that they have little hope of collaborating on their scholarly work with their non-minority colleagues.

■ Clearly Stated Standards and Procedures for Advancement

A professor of color's performance must be evaluated objectively and be subjected to the same standards and procedures that are applied to every other faculty member. Rather than relying on informal lines of communication to convey ambiguous promotion criteria, institutions should develop clearly stated standards and procedures to achieve equality of treatment and to ensure that new faculty understand their responsibilities. To eliminate uncertainty about performance, each faculty member should be evaluated annually and the criteria for evaluation should be outlined in advance. The faculty member should be informed in a candid and constructive manner of the results of the performance evaluation and of expectations for future progress.

■ Special Programs

An innovative way of supporting new hires is showcasing their talents and research on campus and in the local community. The University of Minnesota annually sponsors a daylong seminar, *Diversity Through the Disciplines*, which highlights the research of several faculty whose expertise focuses on issues related to racial and ethnic diversity. In addition to university staff, students, and faculty, the community-at-large is invited to attend the seminar.

These well publicized, university-sponsored events make strong statements to the campus about an institution's support for diversity to the broader higher education community as well as to the public. Such activities need to be ongoing in order to keep the momentum and the message alive. Campus efforts to celebrate the accomplishments of faculty of color as well as efforts to establish research centers to address diversity issues are integral parts of the hiring process. An institution might also establish programs to support new hires in other innovative ways that are consistent with their particular campus context. This is especially important when the faculty's research is unique to the campus, progressive, and/or non-traditional.

2. Assessing the Search Process and Outcome

It is important that committee members and others involved in the search not only evaluate the candidates, but also evaluate the effectiveness of each portion of the search process in order to improve it. At the same time, it is important to acknowledge the things in the search process that went well.

If faculty diversity is an institutional goal and if present search committee processes are not yielding a diverse slate of candidates, then the processes must be changed in order to yield the desired outcomes. Thus, it is useful to examine and understand campus successes and failures. Bernal (1996) suggests that campuses conduct post-recruitment interviews with faculty of color they have hired. Questions to be asked, particularly about the search committee process should include the following:

- What have been the areas of strength and weakness in campus faculty searches?
- How can these areas be improved?
- What internal resources should be added to the search process itself (e.g. added funding to advertise the position widely)? What other internal and external networks should be established?

One academic administrator with a campus-wide view of search committees suggests that the questions below be considered when departments and institutions conduct a diversity self-assessment.

- What is available from the president's office indicating a commitment to diversity?
- What is the regents'/trustees' stance on diversity?
- Are there appropriate university committees addressing diversity concerns?

- What is known about the department faculty in terms of their commitment to diversity?
- Does the college/department recruit undergraduate and graduate students of color? What are the retention and graduation rates for students of color in the university, college, and department?
- When a campus search results in the hiring of a faculty member of color, what were the elements that led to the hire?
- What is the college's/department's record of recruiting, tenuring, and promoting faculty of color? Are there department trends with data covering at least five years? Does the institution have a trend analysis with supporting data (at least five years) showing evidence of hiring faculty/administrators of color?
- Is the external community of color being asked to assist in the recruitment process?

A qualitative assessment of the processes involved in each success is important to undertake. Institutional data on faculty diversity can be collected and analyzed by school, department, and/or division to determine which programs are successful. Search committees should document what led to the hire. That is, what attracted the minority candidate to apply and what finally convinced him or her to accept the offer? By compiling and distributing information on lessons learned from campus successes as well as failures, other search committees will benefit. When searches fail to produce any faculty of color in the candidate pool, it is imperative that an examination and modification of the current recruitment and hiring strategies be made to produce movement toward desired outcomes.

One concern expressed by many department administrators is that there are few doctorates of color in their discipline. If department faculty indicate that they cannot find qualified candidates, then, in addition to strategic changes in the search process, one of their goals should be to increase the number of minority doctoral students in their programs, thereby partially contributing to the solution to the problem. Cultivating students of color who are interested or may have an interest in future faculty positions would be part of the department strategy to promote faculty diversity in their discipline or field.

Even if solutions to failed attempts to hire faculty of color are not immediately evident, addressing these questions and concerns could begin crucial campus- and department-wide dialogues on ways to achieve faculty diversity. Such dialogues, the evaluation of recruitment and hiring practices, and a commitment to the efforts, will become part of an organizational change process toward success.

While current representation of faculty of color remains low and prominent scholars point to factors such as those affecting publicly reported campus rankings as being strong enough to make a difference, search committee members and others committed to the search process can become disappointed and discouraged. However, because success is multi-faceted, committee members must persevere in the important roles they can play toward achieving faculty diversity.

A Final Note

There must be an orchestrated and continued campus-wide commitment to diversity in order to support the efforts of search committees to diversify applicant pools and to hire faculty of color. After the hire, assessing the effort and keeping faculty of color interested and engaged in the institution should be an ongoing campus-wide endeavor. Campus leaders should acknowledge and expect that talented faculty of color will receive other offers, especially in light of their comparatively small number in academe. To sustain their effort to diversify the faculty, leaders must also understand the circular relationship between successful retention and recruitment of faculty of color— one thrives on the other.

Higher education has taken important steps in hiring faculty of color, but giant leaps are needed to achieve the academic excellence that diversification of its campus faculty can bring. It is important to understand that faculty search committee processes largely reflect the level of commitment to diversity in specific departments, on particular campuses, and in the broader higher education community. Search committee processes may be a small part of the myriad of activities taking place on a campus, but they play vital roles. These processes remain crucial factors in fostering institutional commitment to racial and ethnic diversity in the professoriat. A solid foundation for campus faculty diversity can be laid by search committee processes— processes which not only reflect the larger institutional commitment to diversity but which also serve as occasions for serious campus reflection on the barriers to recruitment and retention of faculty of color.

Appendices

A. Checklist of best practices 31

B. Leading Ph.D. institutions of minority Ph.D.s, 1993-1997 33

C. Baccalaureate institutions identified as women doctorate productivity leaders . . . 34

D. Web resources of programs for building diverse faculties 35

APPENDIX A: Checklist of Best Practices

Before the Search

GOOD:
❑ Clearly articulate campus rationale for support of faculty racial and ethnic diversity.

❑ Create a search committee that is enthusiastic and genuinely committed to faculty diversity.

❑ Develop and distribute a presidential statement outlining meaningful steps to be taken to achieve greater diversity among the student body and faculty.

❑ Incorporate the university's commitment to diversity and inclusiveness into campus and community addresses and publications.

BETTER:
In addition to the above,

❑ Create a diverse search committee—comprised of faculty, administrators, and students from both minority and non-minority backgrounds—that brings multiple perspectives and fresh ideas;

❑ Make sure that the search process is also viewed as a critical retention tool;

❑ Require diversity training for all administrators, chairpersons, and staff supervisors;

❑ Include and align commitment to diversity efforts in the institutional and departmental strategic plans as well as the mission statement;

❑ Create open lines of communication with potential faculty already in your department or school—adjunct or part-time professors, graduate students, and research associates.

BEST:
In addition to all of the above,

❑ Secure all resources needed to conduct a comprehensive search;

❑ Make sure that your campus has developed and continually audits a comprehensive plan to address and show a commitment to diversity in every area of campus life—faculty hiring, curricular reform, student enrollment, campus activities, and general campus climate;

❑ Establish and cultivate ongoing and routine relationships with local and national minority organizations and special interest groups as well as with students and faculty at colleges and universities that educate graduate students of color;

❑ Incorporate new research findings and data about faculty of color into the everyday practices of an institution. For example, convene information forums, roundtables, retreats, presenting emerging research and successful practices.

During the Search

GOOD:
❑ Explain to the committee its charge from the outset—a commitment to the racial and ethnic diversity of the faculty must be a clearly stated goal.

❑ Critically analyze the job description and advertisement, making sure they are geared toward inclusiveness.

❑ Mail position announcements to minority groups and organizations, such as those included in this guidebook; university and local organizations, such as minority alumni; and local minority churches and organizations.

❑ Cover the cost of the candidate's expenses related to the interview—hotel, food, and travel.

❑ During the campus visit, make sure that all interactions with the candidate are honest and genuine.

❑ Offer to make available a person of similar background, interests, ethnicity, or gender to give their perspective on the campus and local community climate.

APPENDIX A: Checklist of Best Practices

(continued)

BETTER:

In addition to the above,

❏ Write a position description that attracts a diverse group of applicants;

❏ Contact by letter and phone previous faculty of color, visiting scholars and/or individuals who have made diversity-related presentations on campus;

❏ Establish a vita bank;

❏ Use listservs, bulletin boards, and other forms of technology to announce positions and recruit potential candidates;

❏ Create an institution-wide funding pool to cover departmental expenses for costs associated with the on-campus interview of potential candidates, the cost of advertisements in minority publications, and travel costs for off-campus recruiting efforts.

BEST

In addition to all of the above,

❏ Educate the search committee, and provide opportunities for discussion, on diversity and equity issues, including affirmative action rules and regulations,
hiring myths, stereotypes, and biases;

❏ Utilize personal and professional networks to seek leads to potential minority candidates;

❏ Initiate recruitment trips to universities which prepare a significant number of minority Ph.D. graduates;

❏ Establish a pool of potential minority candidates through a Visiting Scholars, Faculty Fellows, and/or ABD Fellowship programs;

❏ Advise the candidate of any incentives that might be negotiable in the salary package (reduced work loads, grant-funded opportunities, etc.);

❏ Cover the cost of an additional campus/area visitation to explore housing.

After the Search

GOOD:

❏ Honor all start-up conditions mentioned in the final letter of agreement.

❏ Do not overload the new hire with excessive service demands—committee memberships, advising, etc.

BETTER:

In addition to the above,

❏ Follow-up with the new hire regularly to help with transitions and to answer any concerns that might develop in the first few days/weeks/months;

❏ Provide mentoring and professional development opportunities.

BEST:

In addition to all of the above,

❏ Continue efforts to diversify the faculty and other campus diversity initiatives;

❏ Provide the new hire with clearly stated standards and procedures regarding evaluation and performance;

❏ Evaluate the effectiveness of the search process in order to avoid future missteps; acknowledge the successes and failures and share that information with other search committees;

❏ Provide successful departments with recognition and additional dollars to support their operating budget;

❏ Sponsor campus and community-wide gatherings to highlight the research, teaching, and service contributions of hired faculty of color.

APPENDIX B: Leading Ph.D. Institutions of Minority Ph.D.s, 1993–1997 (ranked by number of Ph.D.s)

Institution	Number	Institution	Number
Asians		**Hispanics**	
University of California-Berkeley	204	University of Texas at Austin	105
University of California-Los Angeles	193	University of Puerto Rico-Rio Piedras Campus	101
Stanford University	166	University of California-Berkeley	93
University of Southern California	106	University of California-Los Angeles	92
Massachusetts Institute of Technology	103	Texas A & M University-College Station	89
University of Michigan	96	Harvard University, MA	67
Harvard University, MA	93	Stanford University, CA	66
University of Illinois at Urbana	89	University of Southern California	63
University of California-Davis	77	University of Michigan	58
Columbia University in the City of New York	70	Arizona State University-Main Campus	54
University of Hawaii at Manoa	65	University of New Mexico	54
University of Wisconsin-Madison	63	New York University	54
Yale University	59	University of Miami, FL	53
Cornell University-Endowed Colleges	58	Nova Southeastern University-FL	52
University of Washington	58	Pennsylvania State University	52
University of California-San Diego	56	University of Arizona	51
Northwestern University	54	University of Wisconsin-Madison	47
University of California-Irvine	53	University of Colorado at Boulder	46
Princeton University	52	University of Massachusetts-Amherst	46
University of Texas at Austin	51	Caribbean Center for Advanced Studies, PR	43
Top 20 Institutions	*1,766*	*Top 20 Institutions*	*1,286*
Total Institutions Reported (294)	*5,400*	*Total Institutions Reported (287)*	*4,615*
Blacks		**American Indians**	
Nova Southeastern University	217	University of Oklahoma Norman Campus	27
Howard University*	176	Oklahoma State University-Main Campus	16
Ohio State University-Main Campus	114	University of California-Berkeley	11
University of Michigan	109	University of Wisconsin-Madison	11
Wayne State University	104	University of Arizona	10
Teachers College at Columbia Univ	93	University of Arkansas at Fayetteville	10
University of Maryland-College Park Campus	92	Stanford University	10
Temple University	85	Harvard University	9
Clark Atlanta University*	83	University of Michigan	9
Virginia Polytech Inst and State University	72	University of Texas at Austin	9
Walden University	67	University of Washington	9
Florida State University	63	Michigan State University	8
Michigan State University	60	North Carolina State University at Raleigh	8
Texas Southern University*	60	Pennsylvania State University	8
University of Massachusetts-Amherst	58	Texas A&M University-College Station	8
North Carolina State University at Raleigh	57	University of California-Los Angeles	7
University of Texas at Austin	57	University of Missouri-Columbia	7
University of North Carolina at Chapel Hill	56	University of North Carolina at Chapel Hill	7
University of California-Berkeley	55	University of North Dakota-Main Campus	7
University of Florida	55	Purdue University-Main Campus	7
Top 20 Institutions	*1,733*	*Top 20 Institutions*	*198*
Total Institutions Reported	*6,171*	*Total Institutions Reported*	*747*

* Historically Black College and University   Note: 396 Institutions awarded doctorates between 1993 and 1997

Source: NSF/NIH/USED/USDA, Survey of Earned Doctorates (www.nsf.gov/sbe/srs/ssed/start.htm)

APPENDIX C: Baccalaureate Institutions Identified as Women Doctorate Productivity Leaders

Listed below are institutions that produce a large number of African-American women and Latinas who go on to pursue doctoral degrees. Most are women's colleges and historically black colleges and universities.

European American Women	African American Women	Latinas
Barnard College (Women's)	Bennett College (Women's)	Barnard College (Women's)
Bryn Mawr College (Women's)	Fisk University (Coed)	Barry University (W. Change)
Goucher College (Women's)	Hampton University (Coed)	Bryn Mawr College (Women's)
Mount Holyoke College (Women's)	Howard University (Coed)	Incarnate Word College (W. Change)
Radcliffe College (W. Change)	Lincoln University (PA) (Coed)	University of Miami (Coed)
Sarah Lawrence College (W. Change)	Morgan State University (Coed)	Our Lady of the Lake U. (W. Change)
Smith College (Women's)	Spelman College (Women's)	Pan American, Univ. of Texas (Coed)
Swarthmore College (Coed)	Taladega College (Coed)	Pomona College (Coed)
Vassar College (W. Change)	Tougaloo University (Coed)	Texas A&M University (Coed)
Wellesley College (Women's)	Tuskegee University (Coed)	Texas Women's Univ. (Women's)

Note: Productivity was measured by the proportion of graduates for the particular group of women who obtained research doctorates. The top 10 institutions are listed in alphabetical order. W. Change indicates that the institution had originally been a women's college but had changed.

Source: Wolf-Wendel 1995, 79, 105, 123.

APPENDIX D: Web Resources

The following Web sites provide information on regional and national programs that seek to increase minority representation in faculty positions at institutions of higher education. From providing financial assistance to students and promoting job candidates to creating a campus culture of support for minority students, these resources provide a starting point for further research on current programs to build a diverse faculty.

Black Graduate Engineering and Science Students of Berkeley

http://bgess.berkeley.edu/text.shtml
The Black Graduate Engineering and Science Students of Berkeley helps to recruit and mentor African American graduate students in both engineering and the sciences.

Committee for Institutional Cooperation

http://www.cic.uiuc.edu/second_level/cic_activities.html
The Committee for Institutional Cooperation administers numerous programs that focus on diversity, including programs for faculty development, minority student recruitment, and women in science and engineering.

Compact for Faculty Diversity

http://www.wiche.edu/DocScholars/compact.htm
The Compact for Faculty Diversity seeks to increase the number of minority students qualified to teach in higher education. Program goals include securing multi-year financial aid for graduate students, building a culture of support for diversity on campus, providing mentoring and training for effective teaching, and building coalitions with other national programs.

Consortium for Women in Science and Math Engineering

http://www.nsf.gov/od/cawmset/
The Consortium for Women in Science and Math Engineering researches and recommends ways to increase representation of women, underrepresented minorities, and people with disabilities in the sciences, engineering, and technology.

Hispanic Theological Initiative

http://www.htiprogram.org/
The Hispanic Theological Initiative confers doctoral-level grants and awards, provides mentoring, and runs workshops to increase Latino and Latina representation in seminaries, schools of theology, and universities.

Illinois Consortium for Equal Opportunity Program

http://www.imgip.siu.edu/
The Illinois Consortium for Equal Opportunity Program works to increase the number of diverse faculty at Illinois schools through two different programs, one for undergraduates and one for graduate students.

APPENDIX D: Web Resources

(continued)

King-Chavez Parks Future Faculty Program

http://www.gradord.emich.edu/_pages_grad/ gradstudents/gradstudents_subdir/financialaid/ financialaid_subdir/g_kcp.html
The King-Chavez Parks Future Faculty Program provides financial assistance to students pursuing master's degrees or doctorate degrees at Michigan institutes of higher education.

Minority Scholar-in-Residence Program

http://core.ecu.edu/psyc/nowaczykr/faclgp/ minority.html
The Minority Scholar-in-Residence Program, a consortium established by more than 20 national liberal arts colleges, encourages African-American, Asian-American, Hispanic-American, and Native American Scholars to consider teaching and research careers at liberal arts colleges.

Minority and Women Doctoral Directory

http://www.mwdd.com/index.asp
The Minority and Women Doctoral Directory collects the names and contact information of 4,500 employment candidates who either have recently received or will soon receive doctoral or master's degrees.

New England Board of Higher Education

http://www.nebhe.org/
The New England Board of Higher Education, a member of the Compact for Faculty Diversity, seeks to promote educational opportunities at colleges and universities in New England. The Board conducts a science doctoral program and a 12-month dissertation scholar in residence program and produces a directory of advanced minority graduate students seeking faculty positions.

Southern Regional Education Board

http://www.sreb.org/programs/dsp/publications/f acultydiversity/intro.asp
The Southern Regional Education Board (SREB), a member of the Compact for Faculty Diversity, works with 16 member states to increase faculty diversity. SREB's Doctoral Scholars program works to increase the number of minority students earning doctorates in fields where they are most underrepresented. SREB also helps states establish independent, self-sustaining funding to support the Doctoral Scholars.

Western Interstate Commission for Higher Education

http://www.wiche.edu/home.htm
The Western Interstate Commission for Higher Education, a member of the Compact for Faculty Diversity, works with 15 member states to promote access and excellence in higher education. Programs include the Doctoral Scholars program and the Pathways to College Network.

Notes

1. The author and AAC&U applaud efforts by United States colleges and universities to internationalize their faculties. The purpose of this particular guidebook, however, is to assist search committees seeking to enhance the racial composition of their faculties by hiring people of color from the United States itself. Throughout this text, then, the terms "faculty of color" and "people of color" will be used to refer to persons of African American, American Indian, Asian American, and Latino origin. Asian Americans are included as a targeted group for search committees even though the statistical record appears far better for this population as a whole. Nonetheless, exclusion continues to be a theme addressed by many of these faculty in much of the literature, and the rates of tenure for Asian American women are among the lowest of any group. In the context of this guidebook, "minority" will be used interchangeably with "faculty of color" and "people of color," and be intended to refer to those populations within the United States. As within white groups, there are significant ethnic distinctions within US racial groups. The guidebook will therefore sometimes couple racial and ethnic in the text to acknowledge the many ethnic distinctions within US categories for people of color.

2. The author conducted several interviews with faculty and administrators who have extensive experience with search committee processes and practices. These interviews are the source of this and all subsequent quotations for which no citation is provided. To ensure the anonymity of the subjects, no more specific identification is included.

3. The beginnings of search committee processes are rooted in Civil Rights legislation. What is now known as affirmative action originated in three federal initiatives enacted in the 1960s: Title VII of the Civil Rights Act of 1964, which prohibits race and sex discrimination in employment, and Executive Orders 11246 and 11375, which require federal contractors and subcontractors to develop affirmative action plans. These initiatives were intended not just to eliminate employment discrimination against African Americans but also to increase the number of African Americans in the labor market. Affirmative action was initiated in higher education by the passage of the Equal Employment Opportunity Act of 1972, which imposed specific guidelines for the recruitment and hire of faculty and staff as a condition for receiving federal financial support. Promoting diversity to remedy past

discrimination was further directed to the professoriat in 1973, when the American Association of University Professors endorsed the use of affirmative action in faculty hiring. (Faculty retention was not addressed at this time.) It is from this stream of legislation that search committee processes were developed. Academic and administrative openings in higher education were not advertised nationally until March 30, 1970, when *The Chronicle* began its "Positions Available" feature (Bromert 1984).

References

Alger, Jonathan. 1999. When color-blind is color-bland: Ensuring faculty diversity in higher education. *Stanford Law and Policy Review* 10(2), 191–204.

Allport, Gordon W. 1954. *The nature of prejudice.* Reading, MA: Addison-Wesley Publishing Co.

antonio, anthony l. 2001. Diversity and the influence of friendship groups in college. *The Review of Higher Education* 25(1), 63–89.

———. 1999. Faculty of color and scholarship transformed: New arguments for diversifying faculty. *Diversity Digest* 3(2): 6-7.

Bensimon, Estela Mara. 2000. Forum book review: The color of academic success. *Faculty Forum*, March. www.usc.edu/academe/acsen/ resources/newsletter/0003/news0003article6.shtml.

Bensimon, Estela M., Kelly Ward, and Karla Sanders. 2000. *The department chair's role in developing new faculty into teachers and scholars.* Boston, MA: Anker Publishing Co.

Bernal, Martha E. 1996. *Valuing diversity: A faculty guide.* Washington, DC: American Psychological Association.

Bromert, Jane D. 1984. The role and effectiveness of search committees. *ERIC Digest* 84:2.

Carnavale, Anthony and Richard Fry. 2000. *Crossing the great divide: Can we achieve equity when generation Y goes to college?* Princeton, NJ: Educational Testing Service.

Cho, Sumi. 1996. *Confronting the myths: Asian Pacific American faculty in higher education.* San Francisco: Ninth annual APAHE conference proceedings, 31-56.

Duster, Troy. 1991. *The diversity project: Final report.* Institute for Social Change: University of California, Berkeley.

Farmer v. University and Community College System of Nevada. 930. P. 2d 730 (Nev. 1997) cert. Denied, 118 S. Ct. 1186 (1998).

García, Mildred, Cynthia A. Hudgins, Caryn McTighe Musil, Michael T. Nettles, William E. Sedlacek, and Daryl G. Smith. 2002. *Assessing campus diversity initiatives: A guide for campus practitioners.* Washington, DC: Association of American Colleges and Universities.

Harvey, William B. 2001. *Eighteenth annual status report on minorities in higher education.* Washington, DC: American Council on Education.

Hurtado, Sylvia, Jeffrey Milem, Alma Clayton-Pedersen, and Walter Allen. 1999. *Enacting diverse learning environments: Improving the climate for racial/ethnic diversity in higher education.* San Francisco: Jossey Bass.

Johnsrud, Linda and Ronald Heck. 1994. A university's faculty: Identifying who will leave and who will stay. *Journal for Higher Education Management* 10(1), 71–84.

King, Joyce E. 1991. Dysconscious racism: Ideology, identity, and the miseducation of teachers. *The Journal of Negro Education* 60:2, 133-146.

Knoell, Dorothy M. 1994. California community college faculty from historically underrepresented racial and ethnic groups. *New Directions for Community Colleges*, 87.

Knowles, Marjorie F. and Bernard W. Harleston. 1997. *Achieving diversity in the profesoriate: Challenges and opportunities*. Washington, DC: American Council on Education.

Krebs, Paula M. 2000. Wheaton does diversity. *Academe*. 86(5), 53.

Light, Paul. 1994. Diversity in the faculty, "not like us": Moving barriers to minority recruitment. *Journal of Policy Analysis and Management* 13(1): 163-186.

Makay, John J. 1990. Strategies for recruiting women and minority faculty in communications. *American Counseling Association Bulletin* 71, 81–88.

Marchese, Theodore J., and Jane F. Lawrence. 1998. *The search committee handbook: A guide to recruiting administrators.* Washington, DC: American Association for Higher Education.

Mickelson, Roslyn A. and Melvin L. Oliver. 1991. In Philip G. Altbach and Kofi Lomotey, eds. *The racial crisis in American higher education*. Albany, NY: SUNY University Press, 149-166.

Office of Human Resources and Office of Academic Affairs. 1994. *A guide to effective searches*. Columbus: Ohio State University.

Qualiana, Mary K. and Marci J. Finkelstein. 2000. Promoting diversity in faculty hiring: Navigating dangerous waters. In *Removing Vestiges: Research-based strategies to promote inclusion,* No. 3. Washington, DC: American Association of Community Colleges and its Minority Resources Center, 14-19.

Regents of the University of California v. Bakke. 1978. 438 U.S. 265.

Shattering the silences: Minority professors break into the ivory tower. 1997. Produced and Directed by Stanley Nelson and Gail Pellett. 90 min. California Newsreel. Videocassette.

Smith, Daryl G. and Associates. 1997. *Diversity works: The emerging picture of how students benefit*. Washington, DC: Association of American Colleges and Universities.

Smith, Daryl G., and Lisa E. Wolf, and Bonnie E. Busenberg. 1996. *Achieving faculty diversity: Debunking the myths*. Washington, DC: Association of American Colleges and Universities.

Sullivan, George M., and William A. Nowlin. 1990. Recruiting and hiring minority faculty: Old story, same myths, new opportunities. *CUPA Journal* 40(3), 43–50.

Swoboda, M. J. 1993. Hiring women and minorities. In Ronald H. Stein and Stephen. J. Trachtenberg, eds. *The art of hiring in America's colleges and universities*. Buffalo, NY: Prometheus Books.

Turner, Caroline S.V. 2000. New faces, new knowledge. *Academe* 86(5), 34–37.

Turner, Caroline S.V. and Samuel L. Myers, Jr. 2000. *Faculty of color in academe: Bittersweet success*. Needham Heights, MA: Allyn and Bacon.

U.S. Department of Education. 1991. *National survey of postsecondary faculty*. Washington, DC: US Department of Education.

Wolf-Wendel, Lisa E. 1995. "Models of excellence: The baccalaureate origins of successful European American Women, African American Women, and Latinas" (Ph.D. diss., The Claremont Graduate School).

Wilson, Charles E. 1994. *Development of recommendations to improve minority faculty hiring procedures at Kansas City Kansas Community College*. Ed.D. Practicum, Nova Southeastern University (ED 392 484).

Annotated Bibliography

Institutional Efforts to Diversify the Faculty

Advisory Committee on Women and Minority Faculty and Professional Staff. 1997. Final report: Executive summary [Online]. Available: http://www.thecb.state.tx.us/divisions/ane/Final.htm

This report, issued by Texas A & M University on behalf of the Texas legislature, addresses the widening gap between the state's demographics and diversity in its higher education system. It suggests that the fate of the state rests on how well it prepares all of its citizens to succeed, especially current minorities. Included in this report are recommendations and best practices for linking diversity endeavors with recruitment, retention, and professional development of faculty of color.

Clague, Monique Weston. 1992. Hiring, promoting, and retaining African American faculty: A case study of an aspiring multicultural research university. Paper presented at the annual meeting of the Association for the Study of Higher Education, Minneapolis, MN.

This paper examines efforts to hire and retain diverse faculty. It asserts that the "revolving door" or lack of retention is disabling many diversity efforts. The study examines untenured African American faculty in particular.

Cooper, Rita and Barbara Leigh Smith. 1990. Achieving a diverse faculty: Lessons from the experience of the Evergreen State College. *American Association for Higher Education Bulletin* 43(2), 10–12.

This article profiles the successful campaign to hire more minority faculty at the Evergreen State College between 1987-1989, which resulted in a nine percent increase in faculty of color. Evergreen found that 40 percent of their hires were not in a university when they applied; most were not even seeking positions before being contacted. Good sources for prospective candidates were minority organizations, disciplinary organizations—and caucuses within these organizations—and institutional vitae banks.

García, M., ed. 2000. *Succeeding in an academic career: A guide for faculty of color.* Westport, Connecticut: Greenwood Press.

While arguing that higher education needs to be more equitable if faculty of color are to succeed as easily as their white counterparts, this volume of essays is written to provide faculty of color themselves with information that allows them to be as pro-active about their careers as possible. It addresses everything from deciding on the kinds of institutions to work in, negotiating departmental cultures, developing support networks, securing grants, anticipating the rigors and politics of promotion and tenure, and maintaining body, soul, and spirit in the process.

Gooden, John S., Paul A. Leary, and Ronald B. Childress. 1994. Initiating minorities into the professoriate: One school's model. *Innovative Higher Education* 18(4).

In this article, the West Virginia Graduate College's Minority Faculty Fellowship Program is held up as an example for recruiting minority faculty. In this program graduate students completing their dissertations are appointed as non-tenure track faculty. Strengths and drawbacks of the program are discussed.

Harvey, William B. 2001. *Eighteenth annual status report on minorities in higher education.* Washington, DC: American Council on Education.

This annual report provides the latest data on the progress of Hispanics, African Americans, Asian Americans, and American Indians in postsecondary education. It is widely recognized as the national source of information on current trends and issues related to minorities in higher education, summarizing issues such as college participation rates, college enrollments by race/ethnicity, educational attainment, and degrees conferred by field of study and race/ethnicity.

Jones, Lesley, John Garcia, Linda Avila, Barbara Lyman, Claire Usher, and Marilee Mayhew. 1993. *Strategic plan development for recruitment of a diverse faculty: A report from the EAPS (Educational Administration and Psychological Services) Committee on Faculty Diversity.* Southwest Texas State University. ERIC Document Reproduction Service, No. ED 384 324.

This university report begins with a review of the literature on diversity and the competing definitions of diversity. The report uses an approach that unites affirmative action's focus on remediating actions while also promoting equal employment opportunities and prohibiting "reverse discrimination."

Knoell, Dorothy M. 1994. California community college faculty from historically underrepresented racial and ethnic groups. *New Directions for Community Colleges* 87.

This article highlights the strategies used by California's community colleges to ensure faculty diversity. Topics covered include senior level leadership, awards and incentives, affirmative action, and others.

Office of Academic Affairs. 1996. *The diverse educational environment: An update report on systemwide student and faculty diversity data and program initiatives.* Eugene, OR: Oregon State System of Higher Education. ERIC Document Reproduction Service, No. ED 399 828.

This report from 1995-1996 updates efforts to establish a critical mass of faculty of color within Oregon's state system of higher education. The report profiles the Faculty Diversity Initiative and the need for system-wide procedures to assess recruitment and retention strategies.

Office of Equal Opportunity and Affirmative Action. 1998. *Equal opportunity and affirmative action at the University of Minnesota.* Minneapolis, MN: University of Minnesota.

This pamphlet provides the University of Minnesota's detailed statement of affirmative action policies and their application on campus, in terms of hiring faculty.

Office of Human Resources and Office of Academic Affairs. 1994. *A guide to effective searches.* Columbus: Ohio State University.

This guide provides a thorough list of concrete action steps for search committees and examples of forms relevant to the process. It begins with a fourteen-page checklist for search committees outlining steps in the entire search process, from

organizing the committee to addressing affirmative action issues.

Tolliver, Ella. 1994. *Staff actively nurturing diversity at Solano (SANDS): Faculty and staff diversity grant, Solano Community College.* Final Report. Sacramento, CA: California Community Colleges. ERIC Document Reproduction Service, No. ED 372 814.

This report outlines the faculty and staff diversity grant at Solano Community College in California, which focused on retention and noted past success in hiring minority faculty. Their efforts included: redefining the mission statement; establishing a collegial atmosphere; conducting campus climate surveys; creating a diversity resource library; and training sessions and forums on diversity, affirmative action, gender, and disability sensitivity.

Wilson, Charles E. 1994. *Development of recommendations to improve minority faculty hiring procedures at Kansas City Kansas Community College.* Ed.D. Practicum, Nova Southeastern University, 1994. ERIC Document Reproduction Service, No. ED 392 484.

This study examines the difficulties in hiring and retaining diverse faculty at Kansas City, Kansas Community College. From campus surveys and feedback consultations, the author generated a list of recommendations that focus on creating a climate that welcomes diversity and the inclusion of diverse faculty in campus life.

Academic Hiring Guides

Bensimon, Estela M., Kelly Ward, and Karla Sanders. 2000. *The department chair's role in developing new faculty into teachers and scholars*. Boston, MA: Anker Publishing Co.

This book is designed to help chairs with three important stages of junior faculty socialization: recruitment and hiring, the critical first year, and evaluating the performance of new faculty. The authors translate research into concrete advice and activities; extensively use real-life situations; and provide examples of letters, checklists, and orientations that can be readily adapted to individual contexts.

Bernal, Martha E. 1996. *Valuing diversity: A faculty guide*. Washington, DC: American Psychological Association.

This guide helps search committees assess their climate for diversity prior to initiating the search. Key ideas discussed include the rationale for creating a campus environment that values diversity, reasons to strive for diversity, and faculty self-assessments of their own ethnic, cultural, and ideological identities and how those roles impact their work. This guide also discusses myths about hiring a diverse faculty.

Caldwell-Colbert, A. Toy. 1996. *How to recruit and hire ethnic minority faculty*. Washington, DC: The American Psychological Association.

This guide focuses on innovative hiring strategies for minority candidates. It gives attention to campus self-evaluation/needs assessment, writing job descriptions, articulating expectations, and other successful recruitment and retention strategies.

Committee on Women in Psychology and APA Commission on Ethnic Minority Recruitment, Retention, and Training in Psychology. 1998. *Surviving and thriving in academia: A guide for women and ethnic minorities*. Washington, DC: American Psychological Association.

This guide is addressed to junior minority faculty and focuses on three main goals: assisting new Ph.D.s in matching jobs to their personal skills and career goals; helping women and minorities to maximize their chances for promotion and tenure; and identifying support strategies if tenure or promotion are denied.

Formo, Dawn M., and Cheryl Reed. 1999. *Job search in academe: Strategic rhetorics for faculty job candidates*. Sterling, VA: Stylus Publishing.

This book is a practical guide for graduate students and junior faculty seeking jobs in and outside the academy. The book serves as a "handbook" by covering topics ranging from the application process to negotiating the contract. In addition, the guide specifically addresses assessing the institutional environment to see if the position would be a good fit for the candidate.

Marchese, Theodore J. and Jane F. Lawrence. 1998. *The search committee handbook: A guide to recruiting administrators*. Washington, DC: American Association for Higher Education.

This comprehensive guide is a collection of articles, opinions, and experiences on best practices for search committees that seek to hire administrators.

Books and Articles on Minority Faculty Hiring

Aguirre, Adalberto, Jr. 2000. *Women and minority faculty in the academic workplace: Recruitment, retention, and academic culture*. San Francisco, CA: Jossey-Bass.

Colleges and universities have attempted to diversify their faculty. But their recruitment efforts have occurred without examining the social and structural forces that impact job satisfaction. The author examines the institutional culture and structure of higher education institutions to demonstrate its impact on women and minority groups.

Alger, Jonathan. 1999. When color-blind is color-bland: Ensuring faculty diversity in higher education. *Stanford Law and Policy Review* 10(2), 191–204.

In a legal context, diversity's importance is paramount as a legal base for race-based affirmative action since institutions can use societal discrimination as a basis only in light of present effects of past discrimination at that institution. The author argues that affirmative action programs should be "narrowly tailored" (race used only to the degree necessary to achieve faculty diversity), flexible, cautious, and periodically reviewed.

Bunzel, John H. 1990. Minority faculty hiring: Problems and prospects. *The American Scholar* 59(1), 39–52.

This article charts the evolution of affirmative action policy on campus. In doing so, it highlights how problems relating to access have provided obstacles to blacks earning Ph.D.s. The article also shows how the tenure and promotion system works against minority faculty.

Coady, Sharon. 1990. Hiring faculty: A system for making good decisions. *CUPA Journal* 41(4), 5–8.

The author outlines the high cost of mismatches between faculty hires and institutions and suggests alternative evaluation strategies in the recruiting stage. She recommends descriptive interviewing—giving candidates specific, context-based questions—and teaching simulations, asking candidates to teach given objectives in 20-30 minute period. These strategies can yield better information on a candidate's strengths and their correlation with the objectives of the institution.

Colby, Anita and Elizabeth Foote. 1995. *Creating and maintaining a diverse faculty.* ERIC Digest Report, No. EDO-JC-95-06. Los Angeles: ERIC Clearinghouse for Community Colleges.

Increased student diversity at community colleges requires concurrent increases in faculty diversity. The article identifies strategies for recruitment and retention. Maricopa and California Community Colleges are highlighted as examples of these strategies at work.

Creamer, Elizabeth G. 1998. Assessing faculty publication productivity: Issues of equity. *ASHE-ERIC Higher Education Report*, 26:2. Washington, DC: The George Washington University Graduate School of Education and Human Development.

This volume expands on Creswell's 1995 examination of faculty productivity and focuses on the criteria associated with publishing productivity and how they are influenced by gender and race. This calls into question the use of a "neutral" set of criteria for faculty promotion, as well as whether that set of criteria is equally reflective of women and minorities' career characteristics.

Davis, Josephine, ed. 1994. *Coloring the halls of ivy: Leadership and diversity in the academy.* Bolton, MA: Anker Publishing.

An honest, personal look at the experiences of minority administrators at predominantly white academic institutions. The eleven contributors are academic administrators representing people of color who have faced challenges, crises, and triumphs as leaders in their institutions.

DiversityWeb. Washington, DC: Association of American Colleges and Universities. Available at www.diversityweb.org.

DiversityWeb is a compendium of promising practices, programs, and resources in higher education that provides online resources on a number of issues regarding diversity in higher education. The site offers links to resources which provide ideas and avenues for diversifying the faculty. This Web site began through a collaboration between the Association of American Colleges and Universities and the University of Maryland.

Gregory, David L. 1994. The continuing vitality of affirmative action diversity principles in professional and graduate school student admissions and faculty hiring. *Journal of Negro Education* 63(3): 421–429.

Taking the career of Thurgood Marshall as a yardstick, this article chronicles the major court decisions that have affected affirmative action.

Harris, Percy G. 1989. Almost 50 ways…. *AGB Reports*, July/August: 32-33.

This brief article provides a list of 11 techniques for search committees seeking diversity in faculty hires (including linking merit pay to affirmative action compliance and building networks with undergraduate institutions and professional associations that have strong minority representation).

He upholds diversity as an indicator of institutional excellence.

Harvey, William B. and James Valadez, eds. 1994. Creating and maintaining a diverse faculty. *New Directions for Community Colleges* 87(22): 3. San Francisco: Jossey-Bass.

This volume of ten articles addresses the underrepresentation of African American and Hispanic faculty in community colleges. It seeks to expand the literature by uniting practical strategies and processes from experience with more research-based theories that seek to explain this underrepresentation.

Hoffman, Nancy. 1993. Shifting gears: How to get results with affirmative action. *Change* 25.

This article challenges institutions to shift their emphasis from mere statistical affirmative action data to the ultimate goal of diversifying the faculty. The author suggests that colleges and universities should begin their search process by confronting, analyzing, and interpreting the data about affirmative action. Then, they should modify any affirmative action and other regulatory policies so that they explicitly pursue diversity rather than mere nondiscrimination.

Houston, Marsha. 1994. Creating a climate of inclusion: Success starts at home. *JACA* 3: 146-151.

A desirable climate for diverse faculty and student body has three key features:

honesty and forthrightness; fairness and consistency; and supportiveness. For recruiting faculty, this includes hiring for the "right" reasons (not just to meet a financial incentive); honestly communicating the racial climate on campus and in the community; and encouraging the candidate to speak candidly about their concerns with the position and consult with faculty of color on campus. Retention involves focusing on the individual hired and accommodating their particular needs; encouraging their scholarship, in part by not overtaxing their service on campus, identifying appropriate outlets for their scholarship, and by supporting them in their struggles with racism on campus.

Hune, Shirley. 1998. *Asian Pacific American women in higher education: Claiming visibility and voice*. Washington, DC: Association of American Colleges and Universities.

This monograph is one of a series that profiles women of color in the academy. It is divided into three sections: an overview of Asian Pacific American women; a discussion of stereotypes, biases, and obstacles that exist for Asian Pacific American women; and a discussion of Asian Pacific American women faculty in higher education.

Hune, Shirley and Kenyon S. Chan. 1997. Special focus: Asian Pacific American demographic and educational trends. *15th Annual Status Report*. Washington, DC: American Council on Education.

Hune and Chan discuss issues facing Asian Pacific Americans in the professoriate. An in-depth analysis is provided that highlights the discrimination, including the revolving door, the glass ceiling, and the chilly climate encountered by male and female faculty at various ranks.

Hurtado, Sylvia, Jeffrey Milem, Alma Clayton-Pedersen, and Walter Allen. 1999. *Enacting diverse learning environments: Improving the climate for racial/ethnic diversity in higher education.* San Francisco: Jossey Bass.

This monograph is a synthesis of research which reveals that diversity is central to improving the teaching and learning environment. Students as well as faculty and administrators from diverse backgrounds have more positive educational outcomes in an institutional environment supportive of diversity. Examples of promising practices are provided.

Jost, Kenneth. 1995. Rethinking affirmative action. *CQ Researcher* 5(16), 371–391.

This article from the *Congressional Quarterly* thoroughly chronicles the legislation, court decisions, and popular opinion on affirmative action cases. The article addresses a variety of contexts, including educational and non-educational, as well as public and private.

Klein, Richard B. 1991. Hiring faculty: Broadening the racial and cultural base. *CUPA Journal* 42(1): 23–26.

From his experience at the University of Mississippi, the author charts a strategy for administrators seeking diversity, both in faculty and students, beginning with self-examination and culminating with establishing strong networks with minority students, alumni, the local community, other institutions, and professional associations.

Knowles, Marjorie F. and Bernard W. Harleston. 1997. *Achieving diversity in the professoriate: Challenges and opportunities.* Washington, DC: American Council on Education, Washington, DC.

This study funded by the Ford Foundation examined the growth among minorities receiving doctoral degrees, while noting that there was a lack of increase among the faculty of eleven elite research universities.

Kreeger, Karen Young. 1999. Search committees: The long and winding road of academic hiring. *The Scientist* 13:22.

This article clearly explains some of the "nuances" inherent in each step of the search committee process. Issues of professional integrity and trust are pointed out as important for candidates to consider regarding their potential colleagues as they go through the process.

Light, P. 1994. Diversity in the faculty, "not like us": Removing the barriers to minority recruitment. *Journal of Policy Analysis and Management* 13(1): 163–186.

Departments look to recruit faculty who are similar to existing faculty, thus creating a barrier for developing a racially and ethnically diverse faculty. Minority candidates are there but overlooked because they have a different background than the typical professor in the department. Ultimately the success in recruiting minority faculty depends upon seeking out and placing value on candidates that are less like the current faculty. This article presents a set of fifteen guidelines for universities to recruit minority candidates for their faculty.

Makay, John J. 1990. Strategies for recruiting women and minority faculty in communications. *American Counseling Association Bulletin* 71: 81–88.

The author identifies eight strategies for recruiting minority and female candidates from his experience in the SUNY system. In addition to using flexible criteria, a recruitment team, additional financial resources, non-traditional advertising outlets, and broad networks to identify candidates, he suggests promoting cultural diversity in the community, finding potential links for candidates, and articulating to candidates a clear path to attaining tenure.

Mickelson, Roslyn A. and Melvin L. Oliver. 1991. Making the short list: Black candidates and the faculty recruitment process. In Philip G. Altbach and Kofi Lomotey, eds. *The racial crisis in American higher education*. Albany, NY: SUNY University Press, 149–166.

This chapter focuses on the search and selection practice of black candidates. An analysis of data from the National Study of Black College Students (NSBCS) was conducted to better understand this issue and a summary of the findings and subsequent recommendations are included.

National Association of Independent Colleges and Universities. 1991. *Pluralism in the professoriate: Strategies for developing faculty diversity.* Washington, DC: National Institute of Independent Colleges and Universities.

Institutions need both short- and long-term strategies to recruit and retain minority faculty. Short-term strategies (aggressive recruitment, incentives to hire minority faculty) and long-term strategies (supporting and cultivating students into faculty careers) must be connected to be effective and to demonstrate the institution's commitment to diversity and to creating an environment that will support diversity. A listing and discussion of successful short-term strategies are provided in this text.

Plata, Maximino. 1996. Retaining ethnic minority faculty at institutions of higher education. *Journal of Instructional Psychology* 23(3), 221–227.

This article includes recommendations on how an institution can retain minority faculty. It also contains a table of questions on the recruitment and retention of faculty of color and for assessing a higher education institution's status in recruiting and retaining ethnic minority faculty.

Rai, Kul and John Critzer. 2000. *Affirmative action and the university: Race, ethnicity, and gender in higher education employment.* Lincoln, NE: University of Nebraska Press.

This book explores the impact of affirmative action on higher education hiring practices. It reviews data from the Equal Employment Opportunity Commission and the U.S. Department of Education's National Center for Education Statistics to evaluate the changes in gender and ethnic makeup of academic and nonacademic employees at private and public colleges and universities from the late 1970s through the mid 1990s.

Schneider, Alison. 1998. What has happened to faculty diversity in California? Supporters and opponents of affirmative action differ on the impact of the state's ban on the use of racial preferences. *The Chronicle of Higher Education* (November 20): A10.

This article examines higher education in the wake of California's Proposition 209, which bans hiring preferences in public agencies. The article gives figures on the decline in minority faculty in the state and gives examples of individuals speaking out against using diversity as a hiring criterion.

Smith, Daryl G., Lisa E. Wolf, and Bonnie E. Busenberg. 1996. *Achieving faculty diversity: Debunking the myths.* Washington, DC: Association of American Colleges and Universities.

This volume presents the results of a national survey that examined the employment experiences of recent doctoral program graduates of color who had received funding from prestigious fellowship programs. The author identifies and refutes five myths about hiring faculty of color, in addition to the myth of the "bidding wars." This study concludes that, while the job market is tight for faculty, scholars of color are not disproportionately advantaged as compared to their white counterparts and that opportunities for scholars of color will not change until institutional policies are reexamined and changed.

Smith, Robert M. 1994. Successful recruitment of minority faculty: Commitment, culture, choice. *JACA* 3: 152-156.

Commitment to diversity from top administrators (in terms of programs and actions rather than rhetoric) and attention to the campus climate regarding diversity (including celebrating accomplishments of minority faculty, establishing research centers to address diversity issues and attract minority scholars, and sensitivity workshops) are necessary for successful recruitment. This article outlines several good recruitment strategies.

Sullivan, George M. and William A. Nowlin. 1990. Recruiting and hiring minority faculty: Old story, same myths, new opportunities. *CUPA Journal* 40(3), 43–50.

Cultivating diversity that mirrors society is a priority for all institutions. This article highlights successful efforts to employ more diverse faculty and the need to do away with myths that impede the hiring process. Encouraging recommendations are offered.

Turner, Caroline S.V. 2000. New faces, new knowledge. *Academe* 86(5).

This article argues that higher education must embrace the contributions brought by different perspectives if they intend to continue educating students for the world of work and to provide arenas in which students can interact and exchange ideas with professors from different racial and ethnic minority backgrounds.

Turner, Caroline S.V. and Samuel L. Myers, Jr. 2000. *Faculty of color in academe: Bittersweet success*. Needham Heights, MA: Allyn and Bacon.

In this book, the authors present critical perspectives emerging from their study with the hope of contributing to a comprehensive understanding of issues surrounding successful recruitment, retention, and development of faculty of color in higher education. These perspectives come from the voices of faculty of color themselves, from statistical data collected for the study, and from a comprehensive analysis and synthesis of data presented in the literature.

Turner, Caroline S.V., Samuel L. Myers, Jr., and John W. Creswell. 1999. Exploring underrepre-sentation: The case of faculty of color in the Midwest. *Journal of Higher Education* 70(1), January/February, 27–59.

This article reports on a study of faculty of color in eight Midwestern states between 1993 and 1995. Interviews with faculty point to an underrepresentation of faculty of color as well as conditions conducive to a "chilly work environment," largely created by persistent racial and ethnic biases. The article highlights strategies for successful recruitment, retention, and development of faculty of color within their educational institutions.

Wilson, Robin. 1995. Finding and keeping black professors. *The Chronicle of Higher Education* (June 2): A13.

This article stresses the need for search committees to keep retention at the forefront of the recruitment and selection process. When retention is not linked with recruitment, mismatches between the candidate and institution are likely to occur.

——. 1995. Hiring of black professors stalls at some major universities. *The Chronicle of Higher Education* (June 2): A16.

This article profiles the Universities of Michigan and Wisconsin-Madison, Duke, Cornell, and Stanford Universities to illustrate the difficulties in hiring and retaining black faculty despite diversity mandates and innovative recruiting strategies. It highlights the need for long-term planning to ensure continued funding for minority faculty hires and a good fit between the faculty member and the institution.

Through My Lens. 1999. Produced and directed by the Women of Color in the Academy Project. 15 min. The University of Michigan: Center for the Education of Women. Videocassette.

Describes the experiences, challenges, and strategies of women of color faculty at the University of Michigan. Topics discussed include institutional climate, isolation, lack of community, and maintaining balance between career and family. Successful strategies for effective recruitment, support, and retention for faculty women of color are also provided.

Shattering the silences: Minority professors break into the ivory tower. 1997. Produced and directed by Stanley Nelson and Gail Pellett. 90 min. California Newsreel. Videocassette.

Eight scholars describe how they transformed and were transformed by their respective disciplines and institutions, with a focus on intellectual rigor, academic honesty, and racial justice. This video demonstrates the educational benefits of faculty diversity but also describes the challenges and pressures faced by faculty of color at predominately white institutions.

Guides for Supporting Doctoral Candidates of Color

Bogle, Enid E., Jo A. Blondin, Jane L. Miller, and PFF staff. 1997. A memo to graduate students: Preparing to be the faculty of the future. Occasional Paper Number 5. Washington, DC: Association of American Colleges and Universities and Council of Graduate Schools.

This memo gives an overview of Preparing Future Faculty (PFF) specifically tailored to a graduate student audience. It outlines the aims and history of the program, as well as giving potential participants an example of PFF activities, ranging from teaching about diversity and mentoring to offering seminars on professional issues and forums for faculty to discuss their professional lives. This memo concludes with steps for students to generate PFF programs on their campuses.

Modern Language Association Committee on Professional Employment. 1998. *Final report: The committee's recommendations to graduate programs.* New York: Modern Language Association of America.

This MLA report makes recommendations to address the shortage in tenure-track academic positions and the growing number of "un-" or "under-employed" Ph.D.s.

New England Board of Higher Education, Southern Regional Education Board, and Western Interstate Commission for Higher Education. 1994. *The compact for faculty diversity*. ERIC Document Reproduction Service, No. ED 374 755.

This document identifies five strategies to increase faculty diversity: increase financial support for minority doctoral students; provide multi-year positions to graduate students to integrate them into academic life; create departmental incentives for mentoring and supporting minority students; sponsor institutes and workshops to foster networking and teaching experience; and collaborate with other institutions on recruitment. These strategies require collaboration between different types of institutions and levels of government to align programmatic missions in support of increasing diversity across educational levels.

Preparing future faculty: A national program. Program description. 1997. Washington, DC: Association of American Colleges and Universities and Council of Graduate Schools.

In 1994, Association of American Colleges & Universities, Council of Graduate Schools, and Pew Charitable Trusts created the Preparing Future Faculty program, which provided support to 85 institutions seeking to create programs to improve the culture and preparation of future faculty members. This program description gives an overview of the PFF program, the lessons learned to date, and descriptions of the cluster institutions that participate across the country.

AAC&U Statement on Liberal Learning

A truly liberal education is one that prepares us to live responsible, productive, and creative lives in a dramatically changing world. It is an education that fosters a well-grounded intellectual resilience, a disposition toward lifelong learning, and an acceptance of responsibility for the ethical consequences of our ideas and actions. Liberal education requires that we understand the foundations of knowledge and inquiry about nature, culture, and society; that we master core skills of perception, analysis, and expression; that we cultivate a respect for truth; that we recognize the importance of historical and cultural context; and that we explore connections among formal learning, citizenship, and service to our communities.

We experience the benefits of liberal learning by pursuing intellectual work that is honest, challenging, and significant, and by preparing ourselves to use knowledge and power in responsible ways. Liberal learning is not confined to particular fields of study. What matters in liberal education is substantial content, rigorous methodology and an active engagement with the societal, ethical, and practical implications of our learning. The spirit and value of liberal learning are equally relevant to all forms of higher education and to all students.

Because liberal learning aims to free us from the constraints of ignorance, sectarianism, and myopia, it prizes curiosity and seeks to expand the boundaries of human knowledge. By its nature, therefore, liberal learning is global and pluralistic. It embraces the diversity of ideas and experiences that characterize the social, natural, and intellectual world. To acknowledge such diversity in all its forms is both an intellectual commitment and a social responsibility, for nothing less will equip us to understand our world and to pursue fruitful lives.

The ability to think, to learn, and to express oneself both rigorously and creatively, the capacity to understand ideas and issues in context, the commitment to live in society, and the yearning for truth are fundamental features of our humanity. In centering education upon these qualities, liberal learning is society's best investment in our shared future.

Adopted by the Board of Directors of the Association of American Colleges & Universities, October 1998. AAC&U encourages distribution, so long as attribution is given.

AAC&U is the leading national association devoted to advancing and strengthening liberal learning for all students, regardless of academic specialization or intended career. Since its founding in 1915, AAC&U's membership has grown to more than 750 accredited public and private colleges and universities of every type and size.

AAC&U functions as a catalyst and facilitator, forging links among presidents, administrators, and faculty members who are engaged in institutional and curricular planning. Its mission is to reinforce the collective commitment to liberal education at both the national and local levels and to help individual institutions keep the quality of student learning at the core of their work as they evolve to meet new economic and social challenges.

For additional information about AAC&U programs and publications, visit www.aacu-edu.org.

Please address general inquiries to info@aacu.org